THE ONE, CHILD OF THE UNIVERSE

THE ONE,

Child of the Universe

Human Transformation through Cosmic Realities

Anna Lups, MBChB, MD

Lindisfarne Books ∞ 2024

Lindisfarne Books
an imprint of SteinerBooks

 The first edition was published as *THE ONE of the Emerald Tablet: Illuminating Ancient Cryptic Truths* (SteinerBooks, 2017).

Design: William Jensen
Cover: central image by the author;
background courtesy of NASA

Revised Second Edition

LIBRARY OF CONGRESS CONTROL NUMBER: 2024935922

ISBN: 978-1-58420-871-6

Printed in the United States of America
by Integrated Books International

Contents

Prologue

This book has become largely autobiographical, written from meetings with some of my patients over the fifty years I was in a position of confidence and guiding them in their health issues. Born in the Netherlands four years before World War II and living for five years under German occupation, my primary education was scanty and sporadic. Soon after the war, my family emigrated to South Africa, where I received secondary schooling and, subsequently, my degree as a physician. In 1959, at the early age of twenty-three, "the responsibility for" was bestowed on those taking home a MBChB degree. This is an English double Bachelor's Degree in medicine and surgery, allowing the "holder" to practice medicine in all English protectorates throughout the world.

Politics in South Africa was turbulent. Apartheid increased the schism between skin colors, as well as between the haves and have-nots. Because there was no future for me in that environment, I considered emigrating to the U.S., and received papers to do so in 1963. While awaiting citizenship status, I gathered practical experience in the rural areas of Transkei, South Africa. As a Dutch citizen in the Netherlands, I had undertaken a two-and-a-half-year training in cardiology at the university where my parents had received their medical degrees. In the summer of 1963, I received the official documents as a U.S. immigrant. No threats of expulsion, no green card; America, here I come!

The popular musical opera by Leonard Bernstein, *West Side Story,* reverberated in my heart. In contrast to South Africa, the United States is the country that receives all with open arms. Being a foreigner was special, and a somewhat-European accent added cachet when meeting new people. From the moment of setting foot on American soil, I felt American! This country possesses an underlying hospitality that validates the work of an industrious person.

I accumulated many experiences during the following four years: residency in internal medicine; moonlighting in a busy inner-city emergency room; a serious relationship with a partner; and pregnancy and motherhood. It all precipitated into a decision to strive toward independence.

My search for a home in a quiet, bucolic environment was completed when I became the owner of a ranch-style house nestled in the quiet hamlet of Hillsdale in Columbia County, New York. As a single mother, I was now on my own. The idea of "hanging my shingle" made me ebullient; nothing could deter me in my search for an individual expression and following a dream. As an immigrant, family ties were absent, but connecting with the wholesome witty local citizens was a boon to my life and a constant source of inspiration for the stories I would accumulate. My son made friends and was not shy about crawling over the snow three houses down the street to pursue his own independence. Skiing in the winter was our favorite pastime; injuries, fractures, and such could not keep us away from the slopes, which were just around the corner from our home.

During the next ten years I established my practice, and privileges in the local hospital enabled me to extend influence on a broader range of medical disciplines, including psychiatry, prenatal care, and birthing. I felt a deep connection with the mothers in their intuitive desire for something altogether different in their experience of motherhood. It was a "hippy" culture, but they were successful in inaugurating the new movement of natural childbirth, home deliveries, water births, breastfeeding, and rejection of circumcision. These were all impulses I was willing to encourage, and I was able to assist with at least a hundred births in the ten years that followed. Even now, twenty odd years after that period, I meet young people in the area who know that I was present at their births in a very intimate way. The continuum of medical concern gives them the trust that healthcare can be human.

Mental health care in Columbia County during the 1970s was an extraordinarily inadequate system. The old guard of physicians must have believed that little could be done for a family member who was derailed; confining them to the mental hospital in Wassaic, New York, was not popular. A diagnosis of mental illness could stigmatize and, consequently, was seldom made. It was even suggested that mental disease did not exist in Columbia County. The existence of a mental health society for lay people allowed me to facilitate greater awareness among the local population. Popular songs such as Don McLean's ode to Vincent van Gogh, who cut off his ear a year before his suicide, stirred the hearts of fathers and mothers who needed to know that a greater group of people in similar circumstances did support one another in times of need. My three-year service on the board of that society saw a change in the habit of placing responsibility on the family, as alcoholism and depression were increasingly identified as health problems, and adequate protection was legislated for suffering family members. Changes were in the air.

The acquisition of a second home just opposite the emergency entrance of the hospital in Hudson, New York, enabled greater dedication to the population of the county. I had a strong conviction that the city of Hudson was an architectural treasure in spite of the exodus of most business on the main street. Liberty Medical Arts, as I named my practice located on Columbia Street, was then able to sponsor lectures on local medicinal plants, homeopathy, and holistic medicine. One of the largest events was an exhibit of local painters and their magnificent works in the old flour mill, which stood just behind the St. Charles Hotel. It was an impressive building, with gorgeous spaces for hangings and other art. The artist Fred Harris in particular worked on the space for many days to create a truly artistic event.

At the age of forty-two, a subtle change in my thought and deeds became evident. I heard lectures by Otto Wolff, MD, that shook me to the core. His expertise was gleaned from a spiritual path called Anthroposophy, an esoteric Christian offshoot from Theosophy begun the early 1900s by Rudolf Steiner (1861–1925). Indeed Dr. Steiner, who had obtained a doctorate in philosophy ten years earlier, was asked in 1902 to lead the Theosophical branch in Germany as its president. An expert on Goethe's writings (both literary and scientific) gave Dr. Steiner the authority to form views on modern science and literature. I was introduced to a completely different world of thought, recognizing familiar memories and mental pictures for which I lacked a language. It was exciting and grounded me with a stubbornness to stand by my authenticity. Answers to questions flooded my consciousness. Questions about myself arose: Who am I? Where are my beginning and my end? Is the Earth the only planet with life? Do we live only once? What is the distinction between a person and an individual? Are we alone? And, given my Dutch Reformed indoctrination, who is the Christ?

We are all pigeonholed in the Western society. Stepping out of such constraints takes courage, desire, curiosity, and confidence. Having an abundance of energy, I could attribute to that period a conversion of sorts. I was willing to convert my practice to a discipline in keeping with my spiritual path. As a physician, one could still introduce a spiritual aspect, understanding that my patients needed to sense my interest in their overall goals in life and their dignity of social position, while also recognizing where they had gotten stuck in their individual biographies (a source for their illnesses), and being able to guide them to the possibility of self-healing. (For more on this practice, see my forthcoming book *The Voice of the Patient*).

The following years were instrumental in completing the dream I had imagined since childhood. The times that my parents exposed me to farm life were the happiest. Gathering eggs, milking with the farmer, bottle-feeding the calves, and cleaning and raking—I never had enough. Did I still carry fear for the unrest and deprivation of war itself? Deep down, I knew that being true to spiritual lawfulness meant giving up self-directed desires and embracing obedience to the greater good and familiarity with poverty. Didn't my farmer family live much more simply, and weren't they profoundly happy?

After divesting the ranch in Hillsdale, I purchased an orchard just south of Olana, the estate of the nineteenth-century artist Frederic Church. This was the first step toward creating a space where physical and mental disciplines could be harnessed to strengthen the will. I christened it *Pleroma,* a Greek word meaning "paradise," or "fullness of the Divine." Furthermore, such a lifestyle shared with patients could create a healing environment in which both the soil (through the practice of biodynamic agricultural methods) and the human soul would be given a chance to become balanced. I was inspired by the work of an anonymous writer, *Meditations on the Tarot: A Journey into Christian Hermeticism.* A study of that text made it clear to me that innate wisdom is not acquired but already exists deep within all of us. How can we make ourselves listen?

Then and now—well into my biography, I started the farm at the age of fifty and only recently considered letting go of it. Many patients experienced the magic of nature there, as well as a bounty of gifts and insights. What happened on that farm lives on; it is authentic and inspiring and created in all of us a love for life, freedom, and the hope that life lived is not in vain. Indelible impressions accumulated through fifty years of exercising the gift of sharing and learning from both young and old. Those who bore the burden of altering my life filled me with unforgettable stories.

Most astounding for me as a physician has been to experience the revolution in healthcare—issues of control over life and death, the subtle change toward financial gain so many persons in our field support, and the explosive development in the field of pharmacological chemistry. In general, modern healthcare lacks a spiritual component and context for patients as individuals, yet patients are searching for meaning in their infirmities at a time when beliefs in the temporal and the infinite collide. For a physician who can follow an individual spiritual practice, opportunities to meet the patient as an individual in contrast to *just another person* becomes a prerogative that can never be taken lightly. These become the highlights in a medical career and opportunities to share concepts of infinity and the laws of reincarnation with those people. Hope is connected to the future. These stories are interwoven and presented throughout the book.

Seven years after the appearance of the first edition of this book, a fresh evaluation of the content of **The One** was called for with a second edition and new format. These writings were originally intended as a journal to record the rich experiences of a female physician, single mother, and immigrant practicing medicine in rural Upstate New York. In reevaluating the text, what was intended to be a reflection of an outer journey during forty years of drastic changes in social mores and in the field of medicine instead became a testimony to a spiritual shift witnessed in a patient as a source of memories and anecdotes. The text is a lexicon to the spiritual awakening of the person wanting an answer to physical discomfort. The question resounding from the Parsifal myth—"*What ails thee?*"—is answered not by the medical establishment but now by fellow citizens who, through music, song, and dance, express a healing impulse that embraces the power of empathy and the will to heal suffering creatures and all beings who share our life on Earth.

This new edition, *The One, Child of the Universe,* becomes part of a spiritual-philosophical heritage through which future generations will identify these pictures and narratives as stepping stones toward personal spiritual development.

This book is for the future.

Anna Lups, MD,
November 2023

Introduction

Spiritual Science, as begun in the early twentieth century by Rudolf Steiner (1862–1925), has planted many seeds in our lives. This text endeavors to shed knowledge on the fact of spirit-human incarnation and immortality. Many disciplines, occult and open, ancient and modern, are referenced herein. A base understanding of Anthroposophy, alchemy, biology, and the arts will allow the reader more readily to understanding the concepts presented.

Inspiration from the work of the "Child Artist" is the genesis of this text. For many hours, I tasked myself with the intuition to form many imaginations of his work. Accordingly this text starts with an unadulterated presentation of the Child Artist's work. As fragments from these drawings are presented, I refer the reader back to the original plate, now with an unfolding imagination in context with the specific concept presented.

This book is dedicated also to that Child Artist. After two visits he decided of his own free will not to return. My dedication comes from gratefulness to the younger generation—those who carry knowledge of so much and are unable to make it understood.

Medical science medicates effectively but without real understanding of what happens to the life process of the patient. Authenticity in the young is difficult to accept but is the most precious aspect in our society.

Considerable insight into the *Tabula Smaragdina* (Emerald Tablet) was derived while writing this book. Indeed I discovered that the Child Artist spoke the Alchemical language. This dovetailed well with my own reading and investigations in life. This most sacred of texts shaped the outcome and model for **The One**. I attribute the Emerald Tablet to Hermes Trismegistus, the half-god, half-human of lore (Thoth). Originally translated from the Latin version, I have included it in this writing.

Evolution plays a dynamic, formative force in nature. The folding of sheaths, like a blanket, over and over again, is a theme discussed in detail. Onefold, twofold, threefold—this will go on forever, but in this text I stop at the sevenfold, the point at which the life process plays a formative role in human evolution.

Understanding the Sophia and the Christ as highly developed spiritual beings who supersede the experiences of the five senses on Earth is a task for the future. Evolution of the human being is interwoven with these God-beings, and "doing it alone" is not their itinerary. More often, they will announce themselves and make requests resulting in mental and even cellular changes for our growth and development.

Certainly, this book is about **The One**. My use of bold is intentional and consistent throughout. This intentionality should evoke the reader's personal concept of self, transcending time. Simply stated, **The One** is the timeless Spirit-being, the identity that can incarnate on Earth multiple times. **The One** should not confused with the "I" of the soul life. The use of "I" is also intentional and consistent. The "I" refers here to the soul's response to stimulation and memories accumulated—the Jungian and Freudian *Ego*. The term *old soul* comes to mind as a case in which multiple incarnations have allowed **The One** to shine into the soul life as a palpable presence.

Likewise the use of *Gaya* (*Gaia*) and *Sophia* requires definitions. *Gaya* is the mythical goddess associated with the Earth. Sophia (wisdom) can be described best in this text as the soul experience of Gaya. In a Gnostic sense, Sophia is more palpable and accessible to human beings on Earth.

A discussion of the nomenclature and pronunciation of the vowel sounds is merited. The Continental European and English languages differ, as do colloquial pronunciation and dialects. The same letter having different sounds in context with consonants is also of interest. For example the word *amen* can have both an "ah" and an "ey" sound, depending on contextual usage. It is interesting to feel how the same word pronounced differently can affect the human in different ways. Language is a formative process. In this text, I use only English pronunciations. To avoid confusion, the following letters are used for the corresponding vowel sounds. The reader is encouraged to sound out each of the vowels in times of reflection, as well as when encountering them in the text.

Letter	**Pronunciation**	**Examples**
A	ah	G<u>o</u>d, **<u>A</u>**llah
E	ey	cr<u>a</u>ze, ch<u>a</u>nge
I	ee, ii	t<u>ea</u>m, r<u>e</u>p<u>ea</u>t, sk<u>y</u>
O	oh	cl<u>o</u>se, h<u>o</u>pe
U	oo	<u>u</u>niverse, comm<u>u</u>nity

I also encourage the reader to keep a separate notebook to record impressions during the reading of the text (space has been designed for notes on the last pages of this book). It is always important to write and speak important truths. Once written, these impressions, questions, and new thoughts must be pondered and, at last, spoken in a hushed breath. Truths, when spoken, shape and mold the soul in health. Regardless of religious or educational background, profession or hobbies, it is my hope that this book will encourage you to think, feel, and will out of your **One**.

Finally, when read and understood, this book is a process of initiation—in the becoming. It encourages the reader to become aware—"you are more than who you think you are." The most important thing to bring is your sense of humor, your light, and your curiosity, for they are the stimuli of imagination.

When I was fifteen I discovered something inside myself.

I discovered that what was inside of me was infinite
That one can go down to the bottom of one's soul
And keep reaching and reaching and reaching.

Not only me, but everybody was like that!

The discovery of a quality of super-human power
Unfathomable majesty, infinite existence was part of me, my "I AM,"
With this knowing I could enter my life, my dance"

Scripted from a play, *Without a Word,*
words spoken by the lead ballerina Chrissie
in the movie *One Last Dance*

Gallery of the Child Artist

During my role as school physician in the late nineties, I was introduced in September 1998 to a kindergartner with extraordinary drawing capacities. I will refer to him hence as "the Child Artist" out of respect for his talent to guide us in discoveries that far surpass the natural-scientific mode. His drawings—detailed, orderly, of exceptional accuracy, beauty, and purity—convinced me as an observer that here was a story needing exploration. It was a gift for me to explore the mystery behind those drawings, though they were not penetrated with an adult consciousness.

It should be understood that the following commentary on the child's drawings is based on subjective interpretations. The faces of human incarnations are presented as a journey, and the embryonic development is artistically described. All of these artistic treasures inaugurate the human incarnation.

The Child Artist and I exchanged a weekly dialogue with each other for a period of only three months. During that short period when I was able to work with him, he gave me no indication as to the meaning of the beautiful representations he shared with me. There were no stories connected with any of his drawings. I witnessed him draw, using colors as he saw fit, and at no time was there any questioning or other interference from an adult out of fear that this might influence his pure inspirational artistic flow.

The drawings were saved, to be opened only in the last month of 2014, following his request for a consultation. Now in his twenties, his major study was philosophy, but he also wanted to be an artist,

Plate 1: Standing boy

using computer techniques for his creative expression. He has a history of chronic cannabis use and was hospitalized for two weeks with a psychotic incident in September 2014. After his discharge, while on medication, he reintroduced himself as the boy who made the drawings. Now the time had arrived for those drawings to be interpreted, either to guide him as a patient or to discover if the exploration of this material could be instrumental in his recovery. This book is dedicated also to him. After two visits he decided, out of his own free will, not to return.

Asking the Child Artist for his "identification"—Who are you?—he presented me with a drawing (plate 1). For a six-year-old child, this is a complete representation of a person with hands and feet. The expression on the child's face is priceless, and looking at the mature person now, one can see a resemblance. Observe the courage and friendliness in this boy. Of course, this oil crayon drawing is a spontaneous result following a request and was finished within a few minutes.

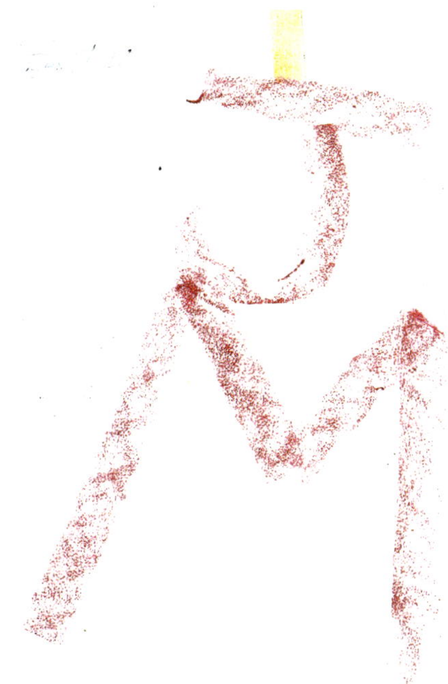

Plate 2: Signature as symbol

After this drawing, he placed his "signature" in symbols on another page (plate 2). These consonants do not represent his real name, but must be the reflection of a remembered past identity or symbology.

Plate 3 (next page) is the first drawing the Child Artist represented to the team of observers. As is customary, using the house-tree-person assignment for the child, we learn about the capacity for balance and the innate connection the child has with his sources of light and warmth. (*For further explanation of this method in diagnostic evaluation we refer you to the work of Audrey McAllen.*)

When the work of the class was handed in, we had no opportunity to examine and discuss the twenty children in the class. Only later did we notice the outstanding figure of our Child Artist. The significance of this presentation was not fathomed at the time, but we all agreed that no questions or interrogation around his creation was called for. Nevertheless, questions lingered in my mind: Does this young being really know what he is drawing? Is he representing from a conscious memory? Or, are his symbols a language he

Plate 3: House, tree, person

utilizes to make contact with a horizontal plane—meaning friends, teacher, and his surroundings?

His assignment was completed as a small vignette at the top of the paper. The house, with a chimney, window, and door, reflect soul balance. The tree indicating his etheric force shows adequate leaf growth. He draws the person not as a human (which we later discovered he definitely could do), but as a flower. This pupil sees himself as a representative of the plant world. Attention is drawn to the figure in the center of the drawing. It represents a tent-like appearance complete with two extrusions or chimneys, one on each side of the pinnacle. There are seven pairs of ribs and a clear division between the left and right sides. On the left side of the dominating tent figure the Child Artist drew a spiral-shaped appendage on the tent. It is attached to the sixth rib, and at first interpretation we recognize an embryonic shape.

Detached from all of this, on the right side he drew a small heart-shaped form suspended in space, separated as an adornment. Here

Plate 4: The Hierophant

he uses red, blue, and green, a combination previously absent. And in the middle of the heart we find a yellow, winged figure—the same yellow used for the flower. Only with an enlargement of this detail does the exquisite angelic being become prominent.

At our next visit to the school, I took the opportunity to meet with the Child Artist again, just to "really meet" him and become better acquainted. It was obvious that I liked his picture very much. I asked if he could make me understand the dominating tent-like figure better, and within a few movements he handed me the picture of this extraordinary character.

The friendly face is capped by a pointed miter that reaches down between the eyes. It fits the microcephalic head structure tightly. The head is not rounded, but carries a heart-shaped, rounded protection from which an arrow-like protrusion reaches toward the heavens. The fun part is the little curly tail that gives an impression of movement. There is no neck in this humanoid figure and arms are raised with two trapezoid surfaces on the ends. Each of these

Plate 5: Metamorphosis of hierophant to house

organs is equipped with a hair or antenna. The right protrusion represents a pointed structure giving room to two trapezoid surfaces, each with an antenna repeated on the left side. There is no ambivalence here! It really is not important what I think these pictures show. It is the viewer who develops an imagination as to what such a symbol could represent.

The story of the Child Artist and me becomes more personalized. At the time of our visits, he carefully listened to my request. Of course, I could not help being curious about where the pictures would lead me. By now I was certain I could learn something that he could convey only through his artistic talent. For the adult, it becomes a symbolic language that associates past disciplines with hidden inner experiences and interpretations. I refrain from interpreting what he shows me as an alien being. This time I want further clarification of the humanoid figure he gave me earlier. Indeed, he can now lead me into the world of alchemical contraptions used in ancient laboratories.

The structure in plate 5 is shaped like a house with four doors on the ground floor. The middle area of this imaginative device provides the viewer with a large window (looking in or out?) and two arms that could be chimneys that also have small windows. The top level has a separate blue window. Is this individuality using distinct colors to indicate different functions? I have seen this "oven" before; it is an alchemical *Athanor,* or furnace. The bottom contains the oven fire. In the middle region, water baths are suspended over the fire. Above this, steam escapes, and adjacent to it an apparatus for distillation is incorporated. The flue area in the attic provides a breathing capacity for the whole. I cannot explain the bell-shaped contraption.

The opulent home with two fireplaces and chimneys is executed by another pupil. No symbolic language is recognized, where with the drawing of the Child Artist the viewer is stirred with memories of the Athanor.

The Child Artist playfully introduces movement to me (plate 8, next page). Inner joyfulness and ebullience are communicated when he draws a conveyance. It is a four-wheel vehicle clearly moving from left to right; the arrow, seen as the front "bumper," clearly tells us the direction. The smoke coming from the back of the carriage expresses speed—I would say very fast—which is also evident in the smoke from the front section, which must be the engine. The flag is waving straight forward?

The comparison between motor and cabin is obvious. The cabin has a door with an elaborate window and a crown-like roof top. The feminine is earmarked as royalty. Merging the male and female elements gives rise to new life, expressed symbolically with the flying birds or the fountain symbol. This drawing has an uncanny likeness to what Alexander Roob represents as the chemical bi-gendered representation.

The difference in plate 7 (next page) is that the oven on the right represents the male element, where the potbellied or receptive retort (*cucurbit*) is placed next to it and referred to as the female element. The "Chymical Wedding" occurs both outwardly and inwardly.

Interpreting the final drawing from the Child Artist is for me the beginning of an exploration into the meaning of this exquisite gift he placed in my hands. As in the Gnostic myth, it involves a

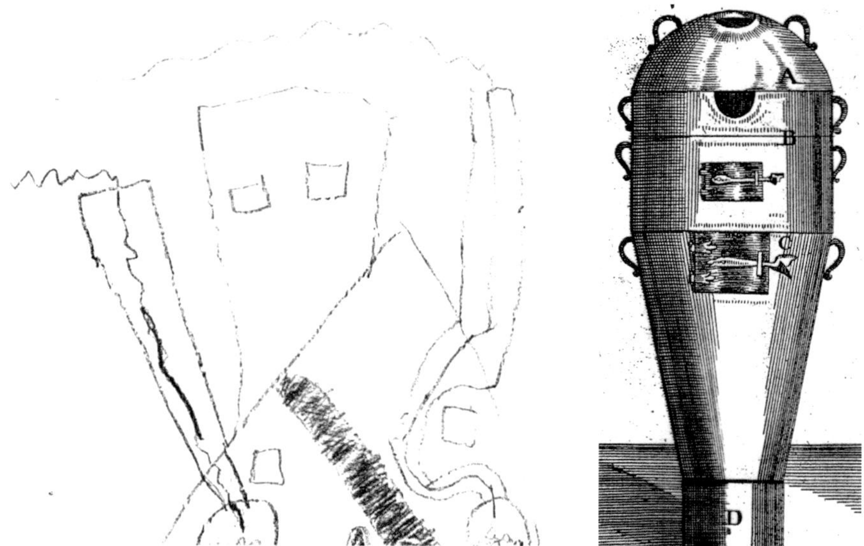

Plate 6 (left): Comparative drawing of home
Plate 7 (right): Alchemical Oven. Used in chemical laboratories, this was an oven in which the complicated chemical processes of evaporation, distillation, condensation, and calcination were observed through a window, enabling the chemist to apply full control; refer to Museum Collections by Alexander Roob.

polarity. The Good and the Evil present themselves in their balanced capacity. Humanity meets the devouring monster and is able to slay it only after many painful sojourns into the depth of the Earth (plate 9, next page). On the horizontal plane, the domain of darkness, cacophony, and false gods, the overpowering jaws can annihilate me. It attacks my life force; it comes to me in the guise of a huge head with ferocious teeth; its small triangular body is chaotic, and the limbs are rudimentary. Is this *me?* The question lingers: Who can be identified as the Child Artist? Still in our midst, how can he be met? Do we want to pave a way to better listening and understanding?

The symbolic nature of the work that the Child Artist shared with me has become clear. Some of the symbols are drawn more frequently in the sketches. I examine the drawings further and identify three of them with the genius behind these simple expressions.

Plate 8: The Green Truck

Process of Consolidation

In plate 10 (next page) we see a spiral, and only the color red is used. He starts the figure from the periphery and slowly wends his way inward meticulous, with balance and conforming to the space of the paper. He repeats the journey inward six times, with only one correction in the first circle. To complete the balance, he orients the spiral by "grounding" it with an anchor, or feet, but does not forget antennae for the upper region. The Child Artist points to:

1) the idea of the spiral for condensing forces;
2) the anchor to illustrate gravity of the Earth;
3) the antennae to acknowledge the presence of imponderable force from above.

The expression of creation as a flow from phase to new phase until the final solid state becomes a reality is represented sublimely in this spiral. The Spiritual Science of Rudolf Steiner introduces genesis in warmth, light, air, water, life-chemistry, and atom. I have taken this sketch as an example of the final solid state, earth, in the genesis sequence of creation (R. Steiner, *Occult History*).

Plate 9 (above): The Devouring Monster
Plate 10 (below): Process of consolidation

Drop-Formation

The centerpiece of this sketch is an exquisite figure that resembles a pelican. Turning the picture around it could also be interpreted as a sickle. Since we have no indication of the proper orientation, I would first like to use the analogy of the pelican likeness.

This bird is used as an alchemical, or Hermetic, symbol and represents "she" who brings her dead young (the base metals) back to life with her own blood (tincture). Our Child Artist uses a display of colors for this picture to represent pairs of droplets—a multitude of them, with five pairs in each corner. Are these eggs? This picture reflects an inherent compulsive nature of the artist, both through the constancy of the five pairs of circles in the four regions and through the consistent choice of green, blue, red, yellow, and brown. In the brown "egg" we find repeated shadowing.

Plate 11a: Drop formation—pelican eggs

Turning the sketch 180 degrees we come closer to the function of drop formation through the cleavage of streaming liquid. Referring to the early formative stage of the embryo, I also call this a mercurial process. The signature that typifies the liquid metal is droplet formation, atmospheric dispersion, and/or condensation. This heavy metal

Plate 11b: Drop formation—sickle

Plate 12: Departure from Sun region

is unique in its characteristics and, in an imaginative way, can be likened to the blood, cell structure, and circulation.

The next set of sketches needs to be considered together as a series (plates 12, 13, 14). Close examination reveals the journey that the Child Artist has to undertake to come to rest in the "grail" prepared for him on Earth.

In plate 12, we see the first stage, in which the Cosmic Chariot has left the "heavenly" home. The symbol for Sun and Moon are on the left, indicating that he is a child of our universe. The cosmic sail is magnificent, perfectly rounded with intricate wiring connected to a rudder. The arrows indicate where the boat will go—away from there to here. On the front bow, connected to a platform or rope-like structure, we observe an amorphous figure that is definitely part of the overall presentation. The cabin is closed. We get the sense that a passive exchange is enacted between passenger and vehicle. The rudder will be discussed in future detail.

Plate 13: Cosmic sled in choppy waters

Plate 13 is truly one of the most enthralling sketches by the Child Artist. It reflects his genius for involving the viewer with his enthusiasm, his control of his vehicle, and the independence he can now assert. As in the representation of the Three Kings, here, too, we are witnessing movement. The waters are choppy; he is definitely "going down" but remains in full control, sitting high and dry in a throne-like chair and handling the way down to his destiny. The sled has no sail, and we sense that the vehicle has become an extension of his own image, a chariot fit for a king. Most prominent is the rudder-like protrusion in the aft, bearing a distinct resemblance to the previous rudder image.

With plate 14, the final moment has arrived. The traveler has left the ship with wing-shaped sails still fully deployed. Could he return? Earthly phenomena surround the intimidated little man—symbols of hearts, fountains, and something resembling headphones. The most important being overshadows the figure—in fact the whole picture is a large shadowy humanoid presence with a very long arm

Plate 14: On Earth—end of journey

that surrounds the little child protectively. No, he is not alone. A guide will be with him to ensure his incarnation as a human citizen. The headphones are an indication that he will become deaf to the music of the spheres. The realization that silence from the cosmic spheres will become a reality hangs as a dominant presence over the sketch. He can establish himself on Earth only by the life force (yellow underneath the boat) supporting his heart forces. Both guardian and the young traveler look toward the right, the blue yonder, as the destiny of their travels.

This magnificent multicolored sketch (plate 15) has become the central illustration for all the steps we will examine in describing the embryonic development. The interesting aspect of this drawing is the two-time division into a threefold organization of the human embryo. First, the Child Artist is capable of reminding the viewer of the threefold constitution of mineral, plant, and animal kingdoms represented in the human embryo. Second, he reveals in the center the threefold organization we find when the embryo divides into

Plate 15: Template for embryogenesis

the three structures of ectoderm, mesoderm, and endoderm. The three body parts clearly indicated to be the upper region as central nervous system, the middle realm with heart–lung (prominently the vertebral *"anlage"*), and in the lower pole a representation of liver under the diaphragm. It could also be seen as an embryonic form; the viewer is free to interpret it subjectively.

This sketch has been fragmented, enlarged, and made to fit many descriptions of embryonic development. The method is scientifically questionable, yet inspiration from his work, as well as a sense of wonder, accompanies me throughout the study of the Child Artist's efforts to convey a message to humanity. What is the message, and can we hear it? Does the message refer to the steps of the Emerald Tablet?

Plate 16a: The Rudder (Plate 13, detail)

Plate 16b: The Rudder (Plate 12, detail)

The Child Artist draws a similar structure for us three times. It is significant enough to reproduce here as a fragment from the larger representation. All three figures consist of a connecting rod, a round heart-shaped body, and an arrow protrusion. The round body connects directly with the main frame. For the moving objects, the curled arrow points toward the destination of the vehicle. In plate 16c, the arrow points to the region above.

Plate 16c: The Rudder—headpiece of the hierophant (Plate 4, detail)

The arrow in the three drawings could have an esoteric significance; it becomes a symbol that the viewer can apprehend while studying the sketches in depth.

Gesture of Dispersion

The symbol for life is displayed prominently in many of these drawings: a spring coming from the earth with gushing water; the many symbols of bird-like silhouettes all indicate this creative process. Moreover, the Moon is related closely to the watery element—not in a literal sense, of course, but in the hermetic vocabulary the Moon sphere equates with the feminine, fecundity the living water, and the fountain of youth.

Plate 17a (left): Dispersion—artesian (Plate 21, detail)
Plate 17b (right): Dispersion—fountain (Plate 21, detail)

I have an imagination that a process of dispersal is presented with this "fountain." From the state of solidity, transformation to a gaseous state is an essential metamorphosis in alchemical work. The Child Artist understood the concept of polarities, or processes in nature that have contrasting effects. I will explore this further in the text on Alchemy.

Gesture of Consolidation

Plate 18: Gesture of consolidation (Plate 15, detail)

Plate 20a: Heart (Plate 3, detail)

Plate 19: Consolidation—embryo (Plate 3, detail)

Plate 20b: Flower (Plate 3, detail)

The Initiation of Kings

Plate 21: The initiation of kings

The figures of the Three Kings were the Child Artist's greatest gift to me and were instrumental in opening my world toward writing down the experiences I had to undergo with the evaluation of his sketches. For years these pictures had been stashed away since I did not know how to interpret this valuable elegant material. A health-crisis sixteen years after he shared these drawings set the wheel of action in motion. The question was whether or not, in my role as a physician, the wonders of his gift after exploration could help to restore his inner balance. Did he need a verification of the existence of the vertical infinite world filled with spirit?

Let us carefully examine this landscape sketch, which is executed in three colors: red, orange, and yellow. What strikes me immediately is that the picture seems to move—meaning that the figures, each one wearing a crown, are moving from the left to the right.

They are experiencing some kind of ceremony that I need to identify. Two sources of "energy" or forces are present. In the upper left we see the Sun, but with careful examination one can identify a being in the center. I feel comfortable to name this source the radiant giver of warmth and light. Undoubtedly, this living being becomes a part of the initiation. The other source of life comes from below, from the Earth, so to speak. Here, living water bursts forth from the center of the Earth. The figures are initiated one by one in a moving order from left to right. The Sun bestows the life, as we know it on Earth, through the gift of warmth and light. The Earth sustains the life with water and her solidity. Together they become the Living Water of the organism imbued with life.

Plate 22: Sun (Plate 21, detail)

So who are these Kings? Literally, are there three initiated figures, or am I being introduced to the "Thrice Blessed King," also introduced as Hermes Trismegistus? Let us examine this further.

Plate 23: Symbols in the Sun

Plate 24: Face of the Moon

The Tabula Smaragdina

Over a period of many years, I was frequently confronted with the hermetic knowledge contained in the *Tabula Smaragdina.* This work is written as postulates in twelve short statements. The turgid writing of Hermes Trismegistus was repeatedly put aside until the Child Artist introduced the illustration of the Three Kings. Was this a subconscious intent? The connection of the symbolic picture with the old wisdom of Egypt becomes the bridge spanning at least three thousand years.

Nevertheless, our Child Artist could not possibly have knowledge of Hermes Trismegistus unless it was through memories from past lives. Because I feel that the source of his proclivity is derived from the resources with which he was born, I listened to his introduction and heeded his information that would become the scaffold of this book. It is the Child Artist who leads us to examine alchemy and embryology, or embryogenesis. The content of the postulate II to XI of the Emerald Tablet will be examined to explain the writings and sketches throughout this book.

We introduce the great mythical figure known as *Thoth,* the deity whose wisdom exceeded all other Gods, Pharaohs, and Priests ruling over that region. He adopted the earthly name Hermes Trismegistus, which appears in the history of the Sumerian people, Hellenistic culture, and Egyptian tombs as a hieroglyph. This earthly dweller introduces himself as "The Three in One," the thrice anointed, the knower of the past, present, and future, initiated with the knowledge of the Heavens, the Earth, and the human being. He was exalted by his students as a being of great wisdom and a master of healing. He became known throughout the ages as the greatest philosopher, priest, and king.

TABVLA SMA
RAGDINA HERMETIS TRI
megiſti περὶ χημίας. Incerto interprete.

Erba Secretorū Hermetis, q̄ ſcripta e
in tabula Smaragdi, inter manus eius
uenta, in obſcuro antro, in q̄ humatu
corpus eius repertū eſt. Verū ſine m
dacio, certū, & ueriſsimū. Quod eſt i
rius, eſt ſicut q̄d eſt ſuperius. Et q̄d
ſupius, eſt ſicut q̄d eſt inferius, ad ppetrāda miracula
unius. Et ſicut oēs res fuerūt ab uno, meditatiōe uni
Sic oēs res natæ fuerūt ab hac una re, adaptatiōe. Pa
eius eſt Sol, mater eius Luna. Portauit illud uentus
uētre ſuo. Nutrix eius terra eſt. Pater omnis teleſmi
tius mūdi eſt hic. Vis eius integra eſt, ſi uerſa fuerit
terrā. Separabis terrā ab igne, ſubtile à ſpiſſo, ſuauit
magno ingenio. Aſcendit à terra in cœlū, iterumq́ d
ſcēdit in terrā, & recipit uim ſuperiorū & inferiorū. S
habebis gloriā totius mundi. Ideo fugiet à te omnis o
ſcuritas. Hic eſt totius fortitudinis fortitudo fortis,
uincet omnem rem ſubtilem, omnemq́ ſolidam pe
trabit. Sic mundus creatus eſt. Hinc erunt adaptatio
mirabiles, quarū modus hic eſt. Itaq; uocatus ſum H
mes Triſmegiſtus, habens tres partes philoſophiæ t
ius mundi. Completū eſt, q̄d dixi de operatiōe Solis

Plate 25: Tabula smaragdina (Latin text)

Hermes Trismegistus is purported to have written numerous tracts, the best known of which is called *Tabula Smaragdina,* or Emerald Tablet. It contains twelve cryptic postulates, which were translated into Latin and widely quoted and studied by students of alchemy throughout the past 1,500 years. Even in English, the true meaning behind this writing was unclear to me when I studied it twenty years ago. Subjectively, I found the statements presented in the tablet somewhat bombastic and obtuse and the development of the postulates difficult to grasp.

THE TABULA SMARAGDINA (English)

I True, True. Without doubt. Certain.

II The below is as the above, and the above as the below, to perfect the wonders of **The One**.

III And as all things came from *the One*, from the meditation of *the One*, so, too, all things are born from this *One* by adaptation.

IV Its father is the Sun; its mother is the Moon; the Wind carries it in its belly; its nurse is the Earth.

V It is the father of all the wonders of the whole world. Its power is perfect when it is transformed into earth.

VI Separate the earth from fire and the subtle from the gross, cautiously and judiciously.

VII It ascends from the Earth to Heaven, and then returns back to the Earth, so that it receives the power of the upper and the lower.

VIII Thus you will possess the brightness of the whole world, and all darkness will flee you.

IX This is the force of all forces, for it overcomes all that is subtle, and penetrates solid things.

X Thus the world was created.

XI From this, wonderful adaptations are effected, and the means are given here.

XII And Hermes Trismegistus is my name, because I possess the three parts of the wisdom of the whole world.

Thanks to my thorough study that followed my examination of the drawing "Initiation of the Three Kings," I have revised my callous judgment of years ago. Here we will introduce the statements of that document as it was handed down from antiquity. The whole document appears earlier for readers to study. It was only through the Child Artist's introduction of the Three Kings picture that I took a renewed interest in the hermetic or alchemical knowledge humanity has been working on for three thousand years without much success in clarifying the text satisfactorily. After being reintroduced to this text through the Child Artist and his Three Kings drawings, I reached another conclusion.

It is easy for modern minds to reject most ancient writings, to judge older texts subjectively in an attitude of arrogance and cynicism. These initiated human beings, wise with the information of the vertical, spiritual plane, were able to convey spiritual knowledge to religious centers of the world dating back to Tibetan, Indian, Persian, and Sumerian civilizations. However, they were still under a mandate of secrecy and were adept at writing symbolic texts.

The source for writing this book is found in the imaginative pictures of a child. Gifts I was able to explore. The tables have reversed; the adult sits at the feet of the next generation and listens. This is a platonic gesture. The child is invited to share contributions from scenes carried from "the past," the wonders of which are subject to future exploration.

How have these impressions illumined the Tabula in acceptable spiritual pictures? First, Hermes Trismegistus states unequivocally that he is offering *truths*. Second, he announces that a definitive vertical path of "traffic" exists between the unseen world above and the sense-experienced, created world below. Next, he points to **The One** as the human being who is Creator. Help from cosmic creators is vouchsafed. He calls the Sun and Moon our parents. Planet Earth becomes our home, where each ***One*** of us individualities will execute and reach for ultimate perfection.

The writer further explains the tools for facilitating the goal of **The One**. Fire, air, water, and earth are the ponderable elements that serve the creative process, first in consolidation but finally return to dissolution. This exchange from above to below and vice versa is clear. And such is the Wisdom of all of humankind that must be comprehended gradually but surely.

Quality of Numbers

One—the Sophia

Medjugorje, June 24, 1981: An apparition occurred in Bosnia, close to the Croatian border and 108 miles northeast of the Adriatic Sea. Six teenagers in the small town of Medjugorje were introduced to a feminine presence, which I will call an "unidentified atmospheric phenomenon" (plate 23). Although all the participants in this chosen group experienced unsettling fear and emotional instability, their visits to a stony outcrop named Podbrdo Hill continued for a few weeks after the summer solstice at a certain time each day, a few hours before sunset. The visionaries all experienced Catholic upbringing, and it was purported that messages were exchanged. According to the local population, the visions involved the Madonna. Worldwide interest was stimulated by occurrences of spontaneous healing and testimonials of objects being transformed into gold. Beginning in 1986, trips from North America were organized. The region of Bosnia and Herzegovina was ruled by a communist regime at the time, and the phenomenon was unpopular with the local government, which did everything it could to halt the influx of tourists. Many photos of the phenomenon can be found on the Internet. The picture included here (plate 26, next page) was given to me by a visitor to the sight in 1986. At that time, Kodak photographic films were still used. It was the owner of the camera who received the gift of "the sight." Her sharing made it possible to announce publicly the new reality of these etheric phenomena and the visage's true identity as the Gaya/Maya, and the "Soul of Human." On examination of this picture my subjective first impression was one of awe and heart silence. How pure this being; how exquisite in her beauty, her mature youthfulness, and her feminine wholeness. Could the eye of the artist ever imitate such a representation on canvas? If so I had never seen a painting come even close to such an uplifting image, an image that fortifies my knowing and full acceptance of the previously described phenomenon.

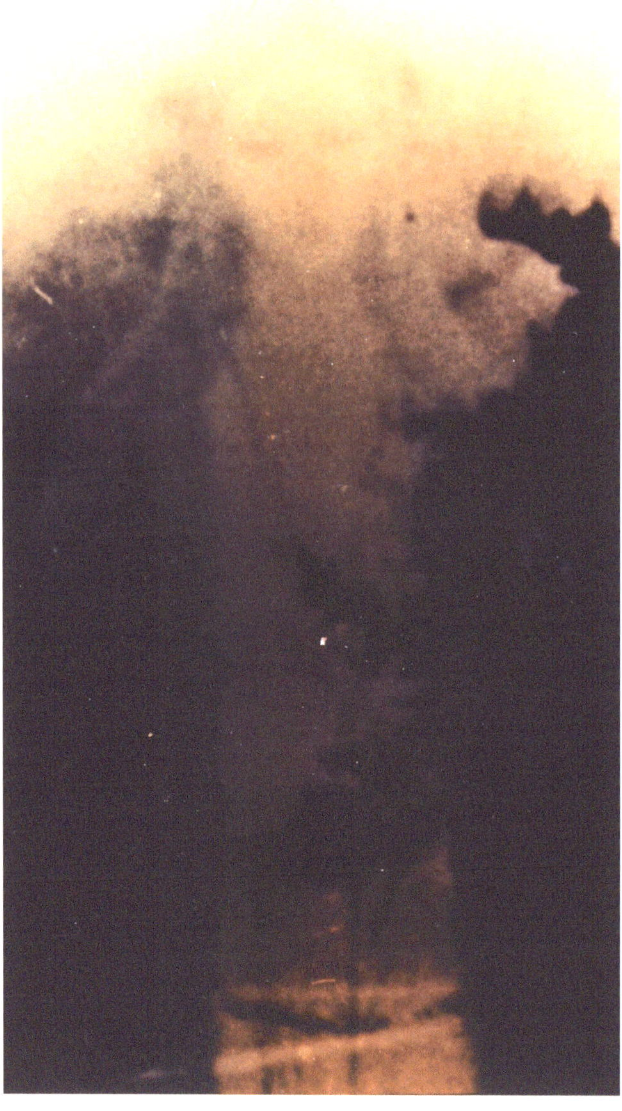

Plate 26: Sophia photographic imprint

What came through on the sensitive photographic film is the "etheric" print of a feminine figure. It is not a solid representation of a woman. The backdrop, seen through the figure, is the mountain as seen from the hotel window. Even the parking lot or a road on the hotel grounds can be identified through the hem of the dress. Of all the pictures taken by visitors to the site, this image is unique and can be seen on many websites.

The visionaries identify this apparition as a holy member of the Catholic hierarchy, which becomes a subjective issue. "*She*" does not exist for the Holy See alone but is there for all of humanity, because She is an aspect connected to the human soul. In our description of the Gnostic myth, we identify her as Gaya.

In any case, the phenomenon of "etheric visions" needs to be recognized as objective fact. More human beings throughout the world have experienced "sights," and in this instance she was identified as the eternal feminine presence who accompanies humanity in its evolution.

Throughout centuries, the Madonna has been adored when intercession in personal life was fervently requested. Visions of the Lady have been recorded throughout the world. A major proponent for these phenomena are the members of the Roman Church directed by the Holy See. Naming her the Madonna is a natural response but incorrect. The visions are seen in the atmosphere and are phenomenologically correct. The content of the atmosphere varies under changing conditions. The reflection is seen in air having high humidity. Reflective qualities of atmospheric metals like silver and gold are carried and make this etheric phenomenon possible. Soon atmospheric visions will not be proclaimed only by the "religious" section of humanity. These unidentified atmospheric phenomena will become objectively scientifically proved; at that moment natural science will embrace the etheric organization of the living world. The proof will be searched for through the pressure of the ordinary person and scientists themselves, who become witnesses and demand a qualitative expansion of the world. More and more people will speak out of knowing, which is also *witnessing*, not mere belief.

Twofold

An article by Katalin Balog in *The New York Times*, "'Son of Saul,' Kierkegaard, and the Holocaust" (Feb. 28, 2016), elegantly introduces the concept that the Danish philosopher Søren Kierkegaard (1813–1855) called *existentialism*. The film *Son of Saul* prompted her to make an intimate assessment of the emotional crisis faced by modern human beings. Kierkegaard observed the growing tendency toward an objective abstract perspective of the world, opposing considerations of the spiritual richness and lawful heritage of each human being. These two radical, opposing worldviews were thoroughly delineated by existentialism. The dual capacity of the human being to interpret the world as abstraction (purely from a horizontal orientation), while taking into account the inner experience of the conscious life, is threatened by existentialism, which emerged after World War II with the writings of Jean Paul Sartre, who stated that each of us exists as an individual in a purposeless universe, and that we must oppose our hostile environment by exercising our free will. Objectivity or subjectivity—both human experiences—were evaluated by natural scientists with the result that subjectivity, intuition, inner conviction, and imaginations—all the rich inner feelings—became unacceptable in the presentation of scientific papers.

To Rudolf Steiner, the imbalanced soul development with which humanity was threatened could be compensated by recognizing that a child enters world existence not with a blank slate (*tabula rasa*), but as a product of reincarnation and therefore of considerable value to the evolution of humanity. Steiner called the extensive body of knowledge that he shared through books, lectures, and drawings "Anthroposophy," or wisdom of the human being. Anthroposophy is a spiritual science and shares a place with the Eastern religious philosophies—Theosophy, Buddhism, Hinduism, and so on. The mystery of the life and death of the Christ is at the core of many of his lectures. Rosicrucianism and esoteric Christianity were inaugurated at the beginning of the twentieth century.

Plate 27: The One, Child of the Universe

Living thinking becomes one's tool in comprehending the concepts in Spiritual Science. The aspiring student must become familiar with the two orientations toward the world. Naming and experiencing polarities, for instance, is the first step toward an imagination in evaluating two worlds. As a routine exercise, one begins by creating two columns, each headed by a noun or adjective for which an opposite condition exists.

The beauty of this exercise is that it affords us the possibility of finding a position between the two realities that reflects a place to identify one's self. The horizontal reality is the physical world in which we live, a reality that is finite and conditioned to our existence on Earth. On Earth, I identify myself as a person with a name, address, position, status, and so on. On the vertical plane I exist but as an individual barely known to myself. Even gender has no impact on my vertical existence. One has to question whether the unknown vertical dimension can be explored through the study of Spiritual Science and how it can be done.

Plate 28: Horizontal versus vertical planes of reality

As we move further into the third millennium, much pertains to functions exercised on what I call the horizontal plane—knowledge accumulated through use of the five senses, memories, and the soul capacities of thinking, feeling, and will activity. On this plane, ever more information is gathered. Memory does not have to be activated; all is obtainable through the Internet. A scientist triumphs through knowledge accumulated during a short human life on Earth. Matter, distances, calculations, molecular reactions in the laboratory and so on, pertain to the life in vitro and to existences beyond our universe. Today we even have knowledge of the constitution of genes, viruses, and prions. We have yet to penetrate the secret of life (*in vivo*) and to create life out of nothingness as only the gods can do. We remain limited to the horizontal plane, limited in time and limited in our awareness of the vertical plane.

The vertical plane, as a different dimension, remained hidden until only a century ago, when the wisdom of these existences was revealed to random members of humanity who were sensitive to auditory and visual stimuli streaming in from the vertical plane. Eastern and Western masters of religious practices have been able to teach their followers about the vertical dimensions throughout the ages, but such knowledge requires rigorous physical and mental practices. Freedom is in the differences between spontaneous information flowing toward me from another dimension and the information I gain from a master. That inner voice I hear still leaves me with a choice of action or non-action. By submitting to the direction of a meditative practice I feel less free but more triumphant with results and information that may be manipulated.

The intricacies of the vertical plane are difficult to grasp for those who remain unaware of or skeptical about its existence. The more I learn on the physical plane, the more my capacities for imaginations are blunted. Listening to "others" requires a capacity of silencing my own voice of judgment, objection, and disagreement. Just Listen! Imagine this! Conceiving this plane as an infinite entity, I experience myself as an eternal being. Time has no beginning, no end. Space is not empty—on the contrary, having silenced my own head-chatter, information flows in and through me; cosmic thoughts think in me. It's as if I become the instrument for and in the vertical plane. I think speech; I speak; I have spoken. The gods have spoken. It would be frivolous to think that it is "*I*" or that *my* thought manifest. On this vertical plane, I become the instrument for the gods' messengers, entities belonging to the as-yet unknown hierarchies from stars, universes, and other dimensions beyond.

Plate 29: Equilibrium of two poles establishes health

I see humanity tapping into knowledge of the vertical plane and wisdom of infinite space, the progression from warmth to life, our role in evolution of humanity as bearers of love and freedom, and the final amalgamation of all humanity to become light bearers.

Placing the two planes at right angles to each other and experiencing my place on each of these planes is a good exercise. The future makes ascent on the vertical arrow between the two planes an enticing possibility. With a controlled soul life achieving balance in the functions of thought, feeling, and will, one gains the ability to place oneself on a higher rung of the ladder while participating fully on the horizontal plane.

The secrets of "the tree of knowledge" will be revealed to humanity in times to come, as may be seen in the younger generations, who reveal this knowing in a symbolic language. My personal experience of meeting these revelations has become a part of this book.

Threefold

The progression of values from two to three includes the awareness that a center exists between two poles. Here we can insert the symbol of infinity that is able to express a pendulum motion, beautifully expressed in our colorful drawing (plate 29).

A rhythm is established with movement between poles. Rhythm is life. Stepping into the living world one immediately recognizes the presence of a threefold order, polar opposites, and the balance in between. In the plant world we project these three distinct divisions such as root system for absorption of nutrients, the leaves for the respiration and circulation in the plant, and finally the flower and seed formation as a method for reproduction. There is an obvious correlation between this scaffolding of the plant and the human body. The Child Artist, when asked to draw a person, draws himself as a flower rooted in the earth (plate 3, page 4). In the following table we can demonstrate that this threefolding finds a parallel in the characteristics of the three regions, so that we are able to identify ourselves as an upside-down plant.

As early as the education in Greek temples, students were introduced to the triangle and the laws that were established out of the subject of trigonometry. The triangle was envisioned as a flat dimension. However when a fourth dimension was contemplated, the student moved into the concept of four-folding adding the next step to the concept of space and depth and the reality of progression to more intricate space-occupying figures (Pythagorean solids).

The spiritual counterpart was also significant for the young students with the recognition that a parallel existed in the vertical world, the world of deities from the stars, where knowledge of the human being presented itself with a unique spirit, personified with character and manifesting in a physical body. Spirit, soul, and body—a division of three. This is what was learned.

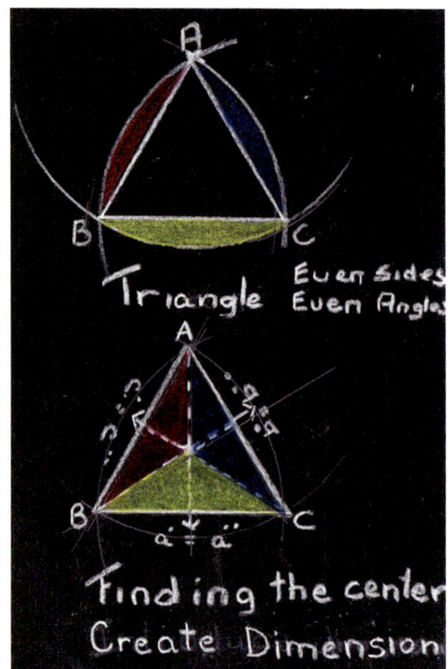

Plate 30 (left): Plant as upside down human
Plate 31 (right): Triangle and additional dimension

THREEFOLD ORDER AS REFLECTED IN HUMAN BEINGS

Root	protection in Earth	stationary	uptake of salt crystals	central nervous system protected by the skull
Leaf	exposure to atmosphere	rhythmic	gas exchange	pulmonary/respiratory system(s)
Flower	invaded by visitors	chaotic	excretion of substance	muscular/digestion/ reproductive system(s)

Fourfold

Standing on Earth, the personal experience of the body is on four planes—front, back, left, and right. All living creatures, starting with the plant kingdom, have a relationship with the four elements that belong to the Earth: mineral, water, air, and fire. The culmination of the evolutionary process on Earth is the human species, called *Homo sapiens*; we are the fourth kingdom. This placement is attained through the capacity to reason while combining the soul-instruments of thought, emotions, and a will to act. While in the process of reasoning, human beings organize their environment, enabling them to establish order. In the evolutionary process, we witness a progression from sentience to intellectual exploration followed by an awakened consciousness.

A cadaver consists of the minerals found in the table of elements. Ever since the time of Aristotle (383–323 BC), Western culture has recognized four elements that constitute the living world. They are called earth (solid matter); water (fluids); air and light; fire and warmth. In Asian cultures, wood is another constituent named as an element. The four intertwined principles present themselves in the animal and human kingdoms. Constantly ordering the living world through the functions of this division lends order in the domain of functions.

Hierarchies on Earth

KINGDOM	EXAMPLES
Human	Homo sapiens
Animal	evolution from water to land / insects, bacteria
Plant	evolution from one cell
Mineral	virus / atoms providing solidity

Through Spiritual Science, we learn that the physical body in its living presentation is suffused with three subtler bodies. We could also imagine that the solid mineral earth body is penetrated by a water body, an air body that carries light, and a warmth body. This is indeed so, otherwise the volume of ninety percent water weight would make us unable to move with such alacrity, ease, and ebullience. The body of water is a living entity and, again, contains within it the fourfold expression of life-warmth, light, tone, and life. Naming these bodies has a specific purpose insofar as the name connects these subtler bodies with our surroundings.

The etheric body refers to life itself, with the water as a means; no water, no life. The astral body would then refer to the stars we identify at night, so that what the cosmic extension presents with its planets and stars imbues us, becoming part and parcel of the emotional psyche, conscious or unconscious.

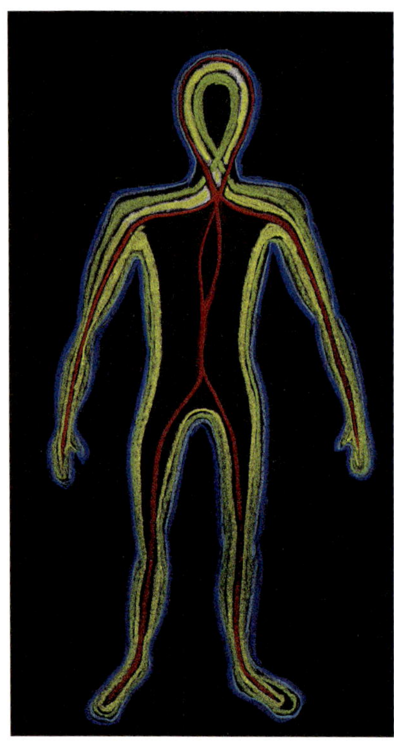

Plate 32: Fourfold permeating body

In addition to life, the animal kingdom must experience movement and emotion to survive adverse stimuli from the environment. Whereas animals can guard themselves from cold or heat, human beings have to develop a skill for regulating their own heat exchange, including the skills for making clothing and shelter. Over thousands of years, the "I" has evolved so that the once-dominant sentient quality has been replaced by intellect and consciousness. Evolution from earthliness to saintliness is vouchsafed.

The Earth itself is divided into four kingdoms—mineral, plant, animal, and human—all having roles in the destiny and hence the evolution of this planet. Past, present, and future are interwoven into these four kingdoms, or hierarchies. Humanity cannot separate itself from the other three kingdoms; rather, they are all interdependent. Human beings are seen as the culmination of the evolution of life on this planet, but the accomplishment of humanity's ultimate goal remains in the far future.

Fivefold

These five vowels (*A E I O U*) have an evolutionary quality. Using these qualities in the sequence of the sections with which we introduce the story of creation as a mythical, subjective experience will help explain the Child Artist's sketches.

Observe the fact that speech in young children is an art that needs to be acquired. When with a baby, adults are always willing to imitate and demonstrate the infant's first words, and we may notice that the words are rich with "ah" vowels in every language.

I have a strong image of how the human larynx differs from the ape-man prototype in the width of the hyoid bone. Not only did the skull extend in size, but the larynx was also prepared as the organ for speech. The first incarnations of human souls had to mold the laryngeal structure and the mandible so that the tool for speech could develop. My imaginative picture shows the air filled in the evening with women's voices around fires, toning the vowels as in a song and freeing the air trapped in their bodies. The children who are not asleep join the choir in a communal gesture of gratitude. The first recorded stories appear eons later, when humanity had evolved to form communities, a multitude of languages, the art of writing, and scientific exploration. All of these endeavors were guided by the centers of religion in which priests controlled information and steered the population into servitude. Members of the royalty were seen as god-humans and were deified, beyond reach, and the ultimate leaders of priests and humanity.

All sounds of the earth, water, and atmosphere carry outward (centrifugally) from the source through vibrations and pulsing percussion. When no substance exists, as in a vacuum, there is nothing to carry vibrations. Water is the best conductor of sound vibrations. The vast volume of the seas is made smaller by excellent sound conduction, allowing sea mammals to maintain contact with one another over great distances and depths.

The ear as a sense organ accomplishes hearing. Through the lymphatic fluid, the ear is equipped to capture incoming vibrations through air deeply within the skull. The quality of vibrations we hear is twofold. First, we can hear tone created by a musical instrument or singing birds; the vibrations travel through air. In addition, speech and sound have different qualities. The vibrations created by the organs for speech (the larynx, mouth, and nasal spaces) are evaluated continuously by the one who recreates the words, hearing the vowels and consonants through the conduction of fluid spaces around the pharynx and inner ear.

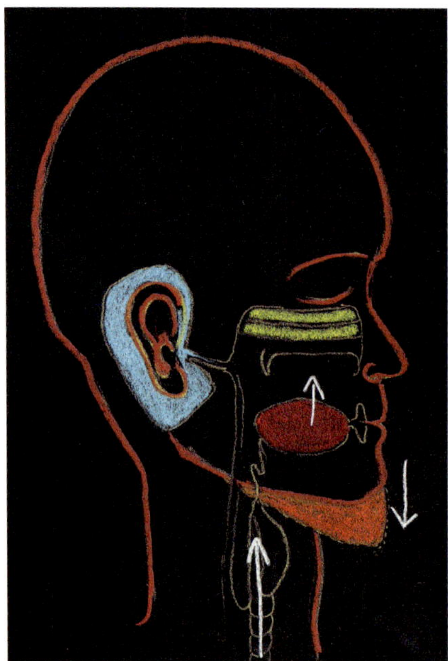

Plate 33: Space for vowel sounds

It is fascinating that the words we form with our speech organ have a dual purpose. Spoken words travel through the waters in my own body and affect the formative forces, also called the tone or chemical ethers of the "etheric" body. Their influence on the finer astral and etheric bodies, including one's emotions, is decisive. Vowels and consonants representing the concept *The Word* are imbued with creative force. Furthermore, speech becomes an instrument for contact with other human beings and has, throughout evolution, been a powerful instrument for building communities and cultures.

All of humanity has a relationship to vowels. Although each language represents the pure sounds differently in writing, the act of forming them remains the same. When forming a pure *A* ("ah"), the mouth opens wide; the mandible drops with the tongue pressed against the lower jaw, and the cheeks are drawn sideways. This is the sound doctors request to examine the throat. With the *E* sound ("ey"), the jaw is pulled up slightly as the tongue makes a platform for the sound to roll off. This sound is often used in a staccato and provides a defensive barrier. The next sound, *I* ("ee"), can be formed by squeezing the jaw and mouth space tightly with the tongue. The *O* ("oh") sound is produced by a hollow space with jaw, tongue, even the palate. The *U* ("oo") formation requires tightening the facial muscles, tongue, and jaw. The ultimate holy vowel is the combination of *A* and *U*, finishing with *M*. This sequence of vowel and consonant is practiced by the monks in chorus and fosters a meditative mood of reverence and a true conversation with the heavens.

As suggested, the vowels work on the human physical organism, which consists of minerals (9%) and liquids (91%). The effect of each vowel is specific, and with careful observation human beings experience a specific vibrational flow in the organism. We have to imagine that the column of water representing my human body is inundated with the sounding of a particular vowel sound, and in consciousness my "I" responds to that experience. With *Ah* sounding, the human body (column of living water) opens up to what surrounds it. What is outside is allowed to enter, expand, and fill me. Its gesture inspires me; it becomes a deep experience of adoration and desire to be one with all.

In the sound expression of *E* ("ey"), a flowing motion is established as an exhalation occurs. I exist as a polarity of right and left and crossing of the two opposites. Through this, I establish boundaries expressed in the warning of the staccato sound "hey." This sound is twofold: streaming and interruption. The point of interruption, or silence, creates room for a new condition. This is a creative sound.

The next vowel, *I*, as expressed in sound ("ee"), has a definitive upright radiating gesture. The gestalt *I* experience is the presence of light flowing from the earth on which I stand. It fortifies my inner being and is expressed by limbs outstretched with inner light toward my surroundings. I raise my lower jaw; my sounding wants to be heard. I AM. I am infinite. I incarnate. I am immortal. I am an individuality.

In the *O* ("oh"), my organism resounds toward an enfolding embrace of the outside world; I incorporate the other. The other and I are *One*. I am not alone. I as a person can hold hands with another person.

The last vowel, the *U* ("oo") sound, is distinct from the other sounds and imbues a specific experience. It is an astringent posturing extension of uprightness. It holds itself contained in my gestalt so that I can reach beyond the stars with my acumen. It actually enables me to extend myself into the cosmic infinity. It is a sound for the future, Utopia, the universe, the commune of searchers, and the sound of Spirit.

Sixfold: Contribution of Speech

Plate 34: Horizontal time element of speech

The human being acquires creative powers through speech. This will manifest as a conscious asset in the future. The six positions of the body and limbs in space convey the connection to the spoken word and its importance to **The One.**

In the first sequence (plate 34), the time element for the "I" is introduced. Here the "I" experiences itself on the horizontal plane.

In the final three postures (plate 35), reaching for the vertical plane in space completes the potential of **The One.**

Past: Creating through the Word

Present: Creating through Goodness

Future: Creating through Love

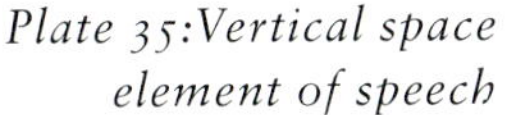

Plate 35:Vertical space element of speech

Sevenfold—Life on Earth

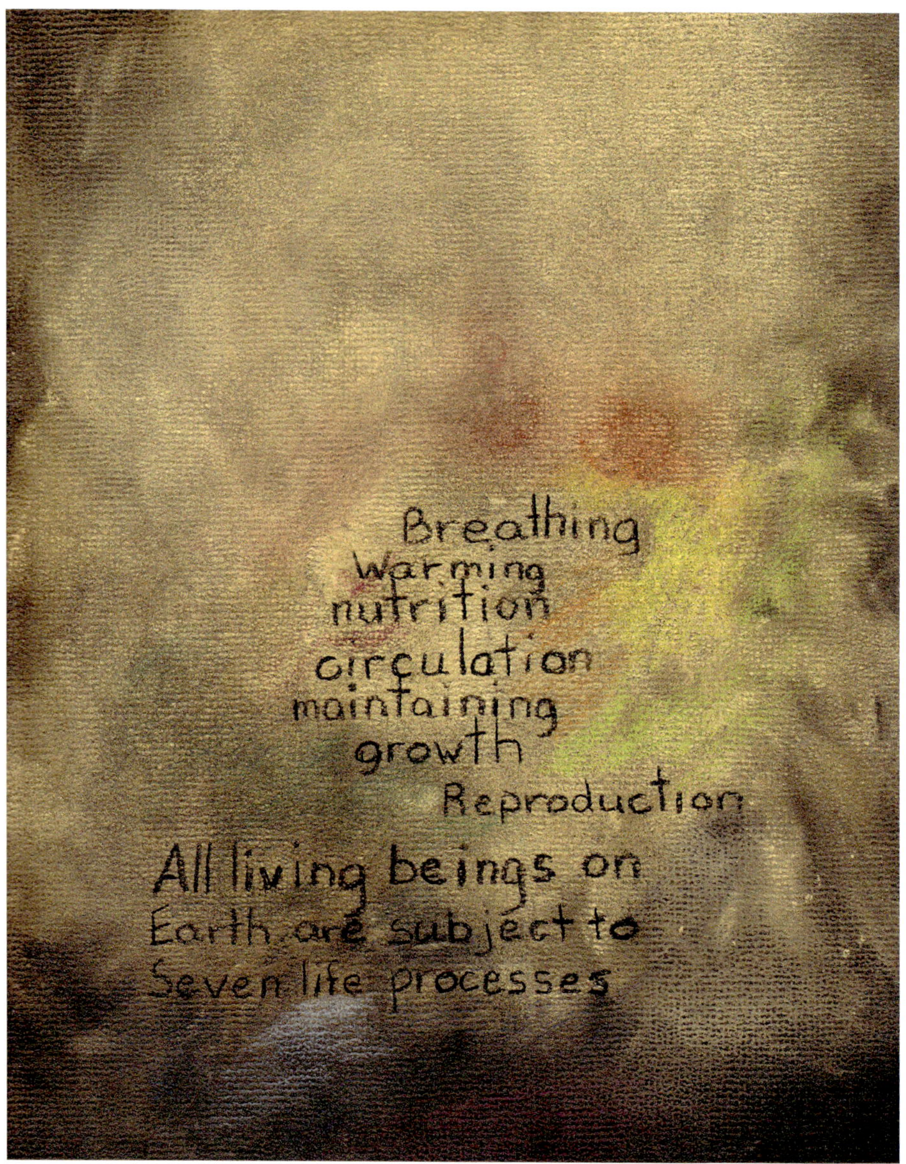

Plate 36: The seven life processes

Seven life processes are embedded in the species evolution as observed on Earth. Our dynamic earthly lives bear witness to this haunting fact. To envision polarities of life and death—as well as the phases between these realities of nature—brings home the ineffability of an environment in which life is not possible. Life is present starting from the human kingdom down to the plant kingdom. On Earth all living cell structures are subject to seven life processes.

In the evolution of life forms we do not see a slow accumulation or acquisition of these processes over millions of years. They are present from the start. Even in the single-cell amoeba, all seven life processes penetrate the existence of beginnings.

These processes are:

breathing
warming
nutrition
circulation
maintaining
growth
reproduction

One can reason that the template for life exists from the beginning. Form and function will evolve to adjust to the environment, but the integrity of the processes is steadfast and no functions are lost.

Was this template *brought* to the Earth?

Could the introduction of the template be performed by the human being for the human being, who after all is the highest evolutionary being on Earth?

Sound A

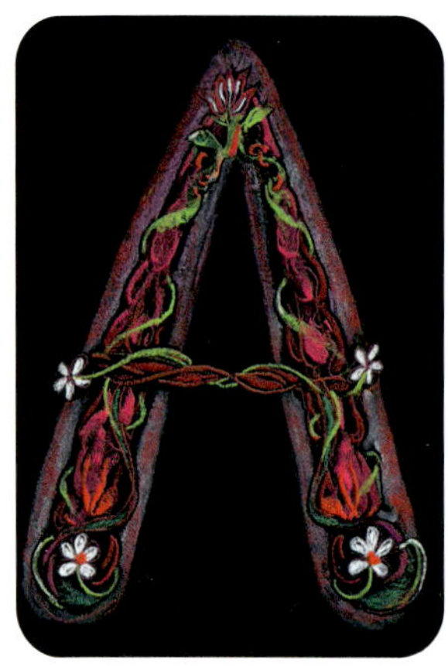

The first section appearing under the energy of the "ah" vowel is dedicated to the first knowledge given to and accumulated by ancient humanity—knowledge of nature phenomena, the secrets of plants and their use in healing, and the domestication of animals to enrich the food chain.

An abundance of images come to consciousness in the expression of this vowel. *Ah,* as sung by a choir of pure voices, is a celestial sound that grounds human beings with a wide stance on the Earth, steadfastly, but able to reach out into the immediate surroundings with slowly raising arms in a gesture of embrace and exultation. Abundance of life, joy of experiencing the Sun's light, warmth found in the company of other beings around night fires—all could contribute to repetitive imitation of this sound through modulation of the vocal chords. This took place in temples and religious centers, where the congregants found leadership, protection, and guidance for millennia.

Among the youth, children with exceptional qualities were invited to join the temple training with a promise of future leadership. Temple science was dedicated to introducing their students to the quality of substances, discussions on evaluating subjective soul experiences during their rigorous studies, and guiding pupils in demonstrating their understanding through artistic representations. The disciplines to which pupils of both genders were familiarized included the secrets of life and death through manipulating nature, obedience to a recognized hierarchy, and the cultivation of nobility. The goal of education concerned the development of feelings of wonder connected to deities, nature spirits, and the discarnate soul of their master. Self-development was encouraged, so that a future sense of responsibility, empathy for life, and emotional restraint would became second nature for the future earthly leaders. Many branches of discipline were embraced.

Throughout the ages, the content of these treasured lessons metamorphosed. What once was accepted with the highest esteem has become scorned as a pseudo-science—*alchemy*, thoroughly replaced today by quantitative sciences, dedicated solely to the physical manifestations of horizontal existence. Pupils on their path of exploration researched the being-ness ("*qual*") of substance, connecting first of all with the polarities in nature—the processes of decay and death versus the abundance of life and growth.

Plate 38: Eurythmy gesture of A

Primitive human beings could choose between two worlds. The still-dormant sentient human soul life was guided by "teachers" in centers placed at strategic points throughout evolving and expanding human population. In contrast to members of the animal kingdom, the human constitution was such that there was an inherent quest to dominate the outer world. It reminds one of the paradisiacal tale—humanity at the crossroads to stagnancy or expansion and exploration.

There were two realities—the rich, protected inner world of self-realization and the ambitious, daring, and stimulating path of discovering new worlds "where no man has gone before." Human soul potential manifested in the polarity of love and hate and in the corresponding responses of attraction or aversion. The existence of contrast became the leading evolutionary impetus leading humankind to prefer and choose the "horizontal" world dimensions of illusionary material possession, the desire to feel superior, and the will to oppress and dominate.

Plate 39: Distraction

In earlier civilizations such as that of ancient India, we find remnants of people with opposite persuasions—the holy men and women and ascetics whose lives were dedicated to self-exploration, inner equilibrium, and the objective reality of higher dimensions beyond the horizontal plane. For those schooled in ancient monasteries, dedication to poverty, chastity, and obedience became the standard for training in controlling the soul functions of thinking, feeling, and the will. Surrounded by a chaotic world of cacophony and fear today, human beings increasingly search for an inner path that promises silence and bliss together with knowledge of higher worlds. Aspiring to attain knowledge or become conscious of an alternate "vertical" plane indicates a swing of the pendulum.

poverty	modest, humble in self	thinking
chastity	containment of emotions	feeling
obedience	following the greater good	will

The introduction of electronic screens into modern civilization within the last fifty years of human evolution is remarkable. Those of the post-World-War-II generation have all been ensnared by screen images alien to reality. The temptations of advertising and absurd entertainment is a welcome distraction from ordinary, daily social and family interactions. So long as such images dominate the consciousness of children, their real human potential will remain largely unexplored.

In recent years, teachers have had to compete with personal screens brought to school by children who prefer to communicate with one another by texting. The desire for entertainment and even addiction to the illusionary distractions will become a primary source of frustration in educational goals of humanity. The use of personal screens and audio devices captures the human senses, which are seduced by images of intense, nonexistent virtual reality. The real dangers of using electromagnetic media hour after hour and day after day by most of humanity cannot be ignored. For many, using screens during their waking hours of the day acts as a distraction and, consequently, a negation and denial of their own powers of exploring the human mind and the development of their own unique inner capacities.

The power of imagination is an inherent human capacity with great potential. Training the imagination of a developing young person is the greatest responsibility of an educational curriculum. It is clear that students trained in imagination will also acquire tools for inspiration and intuition created from their own inner experience. Children who learn to focus on one impression at a time—whether an image, a song, or a musical instrument—will be stimulated to identify truth, beauty, and goodness through the recognition that such human potential indeed exists. Training the

Plate 40: Focus

imagination by focusing the five senses in creating living pictures is essential for awakening and strengthening the capacities of children to explore these truths. Knowledge gleaned from such self-exploration introduces the vertical plane, that involves knowing instead of recalling information from accumulated facts.

Isn't all of humanity given the key to exploring an inner world, young and old alike? On this plane there are no favorites, no aristocracy, no hierarchy. Through dialogue, conversation on this plane is established between asking the question and waiting in silent expectation for an answer.

These are times when even objective realities have become illusory and alien to human beings. By questioning and listening to answers in silence, dialogue with the world beyond the senses can unfold. Given that the tool of silent focus on an image results in answers flowing toward us as inspirations and intuitions, human understanding and acceptance of the vertical plane is not very far in the future.

Educators need to become clear that available resources and methods in the early twenty-first century are significant and that the imaginative powers of children need to be enabled and encouraged. After being held back for thousands of years, such resources from the heavens are again available to humankind.

The extraordinary human potential seen in our incarnating children (the Child Artist) can give rise not only to memories and experiences from pre-earthly existences and suprasensory realms, but can also give humanity an opportunity to weave the potential for love and freedom as a leitmotiv throughout the story of civilization.

Alchemy as the First Science

For centuries, the "language" of the alchemist was silent speech. Through illustrations, hieroglyphs, symbols, planetary and zodiacal references, and the use of color designs and phonetics, an attempt was made to approach the human senses through visual stimuli so that intuitive insights into nature and human connections could be awakened.

The body of knowledge called *alchemy* reaches back at least five thousand years into antiquity, to the Chinese culture of the Yellow King and to the Sumerian culture of Ur. Cultural archives provide vivid descriptions of the mighty King Gilgamesh, who vanquished enemies and eternally befriended Enkidu–Eabani, who as a demigod was master of plant and animal kingdoms. The body of science emerging in the Egyptian temples was secret wisdom called *kemy,* a term that may be found in hieroglyphs on Egyptian buildings and tombs. The actual meaning of this noun, as with most hieroglyphs, could be interpreted in more than one way. It is sufficient to mention three: the literal, the descriptive and flowery, and the secret and symbolic. In the literal sense, *kemy* alludes to the black rich soil found around the Nile River. A deeper, more esoteric meaning understood and embraced by the initiated temple scholars is *"something not seen—building blocks for the substances and objects that surround us."* The occult meaning must still elude us.

A thousand years later, with the rise of the cultures around the Mediterranean and a strong Saracen influence, the prefix *al* (as in *Allah*) was added. After 3,000 years of practice, study, and investigation, alchemy is now seen as a primitive form of science that nevertheless contributed to the development of modern chemistry and medicine. The prerequisite for students of alchemy was a combination of technical skill, obedience to the rule of secrecy, desire and curiosity for the unrevealed wonders of the universe, and lifelong dedication to the subjects investigated. The initiation of alchemy students included honing hidden capacities of vivid imaginations and listening in silence to inspirations of the gods, leading to intuitions that enrich human knowledge.

With the emergence of intellectual soul capacities, the curriculum was expanded; universities replaced temples for training, and the seven arts were inaugurated. This was a gain for young people, but also a loss for the inner capacities of imagination and the higher senses of inspiration and intuition. Initiation into knowledge and overextension of the thought process replaced the capacity for silence and listening to the gods conversing. Initiations were relegated to the religious orders, which instituted a separation of the sexes. Throughout the ages, few women were allowed to participate in studies of the seen or the unseen. Why?

During the pre-Christian era, all wisdom pertaining to nature phenomena, star wisdom, healing, and humanities was held within temple walls. It was secret and available only to appointed residents in those communities of scholars. The temples and the knowledge disclosed were under the protection of deities recognized by gender. The process of initiation could take years in the scholar's life, but after leaving the community the initiate was strictly forbidden to divulge temple knowledge to anyone in the outside world. As an initiate, Socrates was accused of teaching the young men of Athens, and he submitted to the consequent sentence of death by poison.

We have to wonder about the nature of these secret lessons. Most of what those teachers had to say is today part of the normal curricula of most elementary schools and can be found as Wikipedia entries and in numerous other sources. When young children are allowed to ponder the environment and the processes of nature around them, they can develop feelings of awe and be stimulated by curiosity to experience the satisfaction of observing and understanding. Instead of relying on the memory and rote learning methods, children can develop through active participation in exchanges between teacher and student. This interaction is a platonic form of pedagogy whereby the pupil can become the teacher and we learn from one another regardless of age, gender, or status.

The many drawings made by the six-year-old "Child Artist" demonstrate such a platonic exchange. The topic chosen by the young artist demonstrates his "knowing" of basic nature processes. The imaginations he shares reveal intimate familiarity with alchemical laws and introduce us to the advanced soul of a once-eminent mind, encouraging us to ask: Who are we meeting? Who teaches Us?

Processes in Nature

The expression of water under changing atmospheric conditions becomes a tool for grasping the processes of nature and the idea of metamorphosis of substance. When cold enough, the H_2O molecule changes to a crystalline state. Snowflakes—brilliant stars uniquely formed in a six-arm configuration—fall from the sky in a fixed condition, embracing the Earth surface with a dusting of white salt. In the alchemist's laboratory, this was called the *salt process*—an activity of consolidation and crystal formation in a cold, dry environment.

Plate 41: Snowflake

Plate 42: Cumulus cloud

Ice is a solid, stone-like substance with the same molecule as water. The heat of the Sun and warmer weather melts the solid ice into water. The activity of H_2O molecules change to become

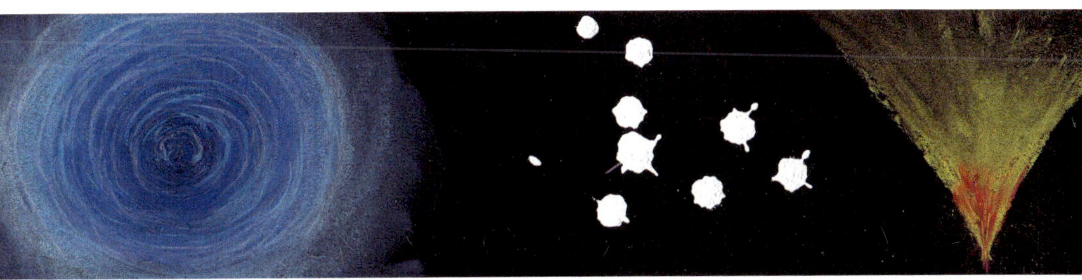

Plate 43: Salt mercury sulfur process

livelier, and the liquid state is introduced. Warmth brings H_2O into a solution, also called the *solvent* process.

In nature, the atmosphere stimulates evaporation, and droplets disperse and move upward against the gravitational draw of the Earth to form clouds. A child can look up to the sky and be one with the bellowing towering white (ac)cumulus of water. In a kitchen, it is steam from the kettle; in nature it becomes fog and clouds. In the fog state, humidity penetrates throughout the atmosphere in a cloying repulsive fashion, resembling the putrid sulfuric odor of a decaying product. When the dispersal process of nature takes place in a laboratory, it is called a *sulfur* process.

What do we find between these two poles of salt formation and the sulfur process of dispersion? In a laboratory this is the process of droplet formation, and is seen in nature as dew drops or rain. It is referred to as the *mercury* process.

Every child knows the words *snow, rain,* and *fog* at an early age, and these words form pictures in children's minds and become parts of their imagination. The processes of evaporation followed by condensation are procedures executed in the laboratory and practiced by alchemists to derive the substances they desire. Pupils become acquainted with the chemical characteristics of salt, mercury, and sulfur.

In the drawings of the Child Artist, these basic natural processes are distinctly identified, indicating familiarity with the alchemical designations of salt formation, drop formation, and dispersion by way of gas or air. When questioning the mature Child Artist today about the significance of these images, he had no recognition of his own work. This proves to me that his process as the Child Artist belongs to his unconscious, hidden memory—clearly not connecting him to the stage of his life he is now experiencing. Although not penetrated into the Child Artist's consciousness, the exchange between the two of us is an example of platonic teaching, whereby I received and could interpret the mysterious, symbolic content of the drawings he presented. In further drawings, my choice of investigating alchemy in more depth will become very clear.

Alchemical process	salt	mercury	sulfur
Interpretation of Child Artist	spiral	eggs	fountain
Associated force	centripetal	balance	centrifugal
Presentation in nature	crystal	drop	vapor
Phase	solid	liquid	gas

The next step for a pupil in the temple training was to find the combination of these three processes of nature in one living form. This archetype is represented in the threefold structure of the plant—root, leaf, and flower. The root system is dominated by salt formation, the leaf system by the mercury processes, and the flower structure equates to the sulfur process, whereby it surrounds the reproductive organ of the plant to attract life forms helping in pollination. As a summary I have combined these three phenomena in nature, so that a distinct function can be appreciated.

Threefold Function in the Human Form

Liberty Hyde Bailey (1858–1954), a well-known American scholar, horticulturist, and author of *The Holy Earth* (1915), dedicated the last third of his life to social concerns of American youth and created the 4H movement, in which *Head, Heart, Hand* and

Health indicated the need for striking a balance in the lives of teenagers. While living in Hillsdale, New York (1972), I was asked to become a 4H leader of the local girls, setting examples in housekeeping, sewing, nutrition, and rhythm in daily life. Being fastidious, this was right up my alley, but I wasn't able to keep up with that busy life for more than a year. That was long enough, however, to encounter this respected scholar through his writings and to marvel at the wisdom of his ideas.

Balance of function in the three different parts of the body—the head for thinking, the heart for feeling, and the hand for will activity—brought home to me how important it is to distinguish the body's separation into three segments. Strangely enough, this scaffold has not been carried over, and the biography of Liberty Bailey is seldom mentioned today. The archetype of the human form can be seen in the threefold nature of head, heart, and hand, or the upside-down plant.

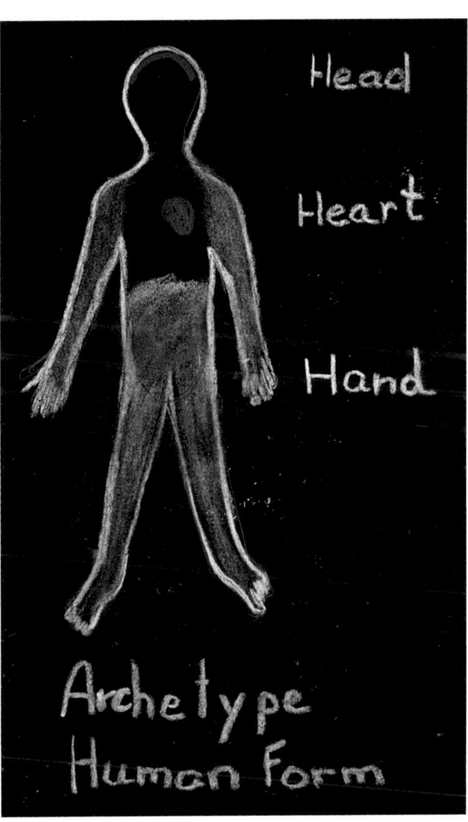

Plate 44: Archetype human form

The content of the skull, the brain, is surrounded by the cerebral-spinal fluid and protected from gravity and sudden movements in a cocoon-like state. This part of human anatomy resembles the root system in the plant—kept in a state of darkness and protected from outside stimuli. The exchange of thought content becomes like a salt process.

The chest region, containing the heart and the lungs, is submitted throughout life to a steady, rhythmic four heartbeats to one breath of the lungs. The mercury process can be identified in the droplet structure of the alveoli and in the blood droplets of the circulation. Like the leaf distribution on the branch of the plant, the rhythmic quality is present throughout every aspect, imitating a breathing process of inhaling and exhaling for the exchange of oxygen and carbon.

Uncoordinated chaotic movements imbue all activity under the diaphragm. This process resembles a turbulent fomenting activity, with the production of sulfurous-smelling gases in the gut. The sulfurous gesture is recognized in the plant in its flower formation. Through stimulation of the senses by the surrounding world (color or odor), the flower display brings the plant cycle to a conclusion. The reproductive nature of the plant uses the atomizing effect of sulfur to complete its procreation with the help of insects. The human limbs, the extremities enabling human movement, are incorporated into the lower system. Movement of the extremities in a newborn child is chaotic; human will forces develop toward a fluidity and grace only with training and the development of coordination. A unique signature is identifiable in the movement of a person.

Summary of Nature Processes and Correlations in the Human Being

process	salt	mercury	sulfur
representation in plant	root	leaf	flower
representation in nature	snow, ice	rain, dew	fog, vapor
representation in the human	skull, head	heart, lung	hand, gut
seat of the soul function	think	feel	will

Three Kings

As a child between four and nine years of age during World War II, much of my education was left to my own devices. Even at a young age, our homeschooling consisted of studying a phenomenon of our own choice for a day and reporting on it at the dinner table. Even an emotional observation counted as learning. There was tension on the streets, as neighbors with yellow stars on their chest were removed. At night, with sirens blaring and the rumble of planes overhead, the three sibling children quickly descended into the dark stinky basement—waiting for what? Yet I had time to philosophize about the numbers 1, 2, 3, 4 and could look at them on paper, each shining with a different color and imbued by a distinct meaning. In this exploration, I could revel in the fact that, although just numbers, they had a deeper identity and significance for me. I loved the number three most of all because, although it represents three entities, I could imagine them having a fervent desire to melt into one again. Two was a split, but three represented the past, present, and future, all wrapped into one symbol. How could I have known then that after fifty-six years, a boy the same age that I was then would introduce me to a new challenge with this mysterious thrice/one symbol?

It was surprising when the Child Artist handed me the picture I titled "The Initiation of the Three Kings" (plate 21, page 19). Careful examination introduces us to two sources of enlightenment for the three crowned figures being initiated. First, the earthly source in the form of the fountain, which we previously introduced as the source of mercurial powers personifying the quality of life through the function of breathing. On Earth, the home of life is the "living" water contained in all life forms. The three figures, each wearing a crown, share the two overflowing sources, but with careful observation I discern a moving quality in this picture.

Let's examine the heavenly body in the left corner. "Oh, that is the Sun!" I say. But look carefully; this orb, radiating warmth (red) and light (yellow), is hollow and filled with a being. The distribution of the three figures is unequal; under the bestowing orb, two of the figures are tardy. One figure has "moved on" and has received "blessing" from the Earth—the fountain of living water springing from the depths. This drawing does convey movement, the experience of the figures on a "spiritual" path from left to right, while experiencing or inundated so to speak with sources of Warmth, Light from above, and Life from the Earth center. This drawing represents a ceremony enacted for perhaps only one person—not just once but three times. Who are the Three Kings? Could the three figures represent one being who thrice repeats a blessed immersion into life, vouchsafed by earthly wisdoms?

Plate 45: Three Kings (reproduced)

The reintroduction of Three Kings as the lofty Hermes Trismegistus, together with the opportunity to reconsider his postulates in the form of the *Tabula Smaragdina,* becomes a new imagination that combines the work of the Master with one of his pupils, the Child

Artist. The teachings in the Tabula draw attention to the physical incarnation of the human being in a step wise construction of the embryonic body. He conveys the magnitude of **The One** being the human embryonic presence. He continues to mention the contributions of the four cosmic regions (*sun, moon, air, and earth*), that augment (perfuse) the solid constitution derived from the reproductive cells of the parents. He declares himself as the master of knowing these reproductive processes with unassailable certainty.

In the Child Artist, we discover two illustrations that lead us into the imaginative world of past knowing. First, the wonderful initiation of the Three Kings, which acquaints us with the *Tabula Smaragdina*. Second, the one truthful illustration involving the stages in embryonic development. These are the stepping stones on which I can build my hypothesis of the wonders of **The One** and thereby also awaken the authenticity and hopeful future in my own biography.

Revisiting the emerald tablet becomes the goal in this biography. With the illustrations of the Child Artist, I am able to explore a meaningful discussion of the postulates in section E (ey), which includes drawings of embryological forms.

Alchemical Equipment

The pictures of the Child Artist continue to take us on a journey. The secret codes and drawings he shares are filled with riddles and conceal truths. For the student and interpreter the challenge remains in how far we have understood the language. In visiting the "master" in his schooling of Alchemy he was generous to share indications of equipment used in the laboratories of old. The outstanding example is the Green Truck drawing, for which we found an excellent comparative in Roob as demonstrated here.

Plate 46: Reproduction of Green Truck for comparison to alchemical equipment

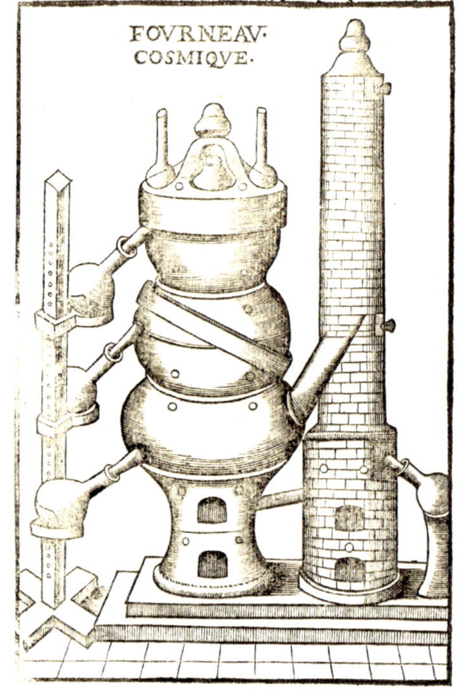

The Path of Initiation for the Alchemist

Considering the thousands of years that the discipline of Hermetic science, or Alchemy, has influenced learned men and women, I have become convinced that Gnostic myths played a definitive role in soul development of many of those students. Those myths will play a role in the Genesis story that unfolds in the next section, when both the biblical Genesis and embryogenesis are illumined. For alchemical students on a path of initiation, elements of dark matter in their own soul life needed to be expunged, undergo sublimation, and be transformed into *lapis,* to return into the paradisiacal primordial state. Finding the correct pathway was a chief concern and this secret was protected throughout the ages by code names, symbols, and illustrations. Clearly, a guide or master was still needed. The journey required passing through the outermost circle of the underworld, a world filled with monsters and beastly creatures, a world so frightening that only by conjuring up courage and with the help of the divine world was a student able to complete the task. Enlightenment does not come without hurdles.

Plate 47: Return of the Devouring Monster

The Monster presented in the Gallery (plate 9, page 10) calls for a conclusion of the Child Artist's work. Like a mythical Seth, this fierce monster devours all that is alive and leaves chaos and destruction in its wake. Hope and courage are the two contributions attained by the graduate and the promise of a meaningful future for Earth and humanity.

Sound E

In this chapter we encounter a gesture that lives in the duality of a short staccato followed by an uninterrupted, longer, transformed circular movement. Throughout space the short exclamation of E (ey) forcefully interferes with the primary centrifugal flowing of the A (ah) gesture. This crossing brings the possibility of change in existing dynamic flow. Together with the perseverance in the turbulence and seeming chaos created during this confrontation is the experience of a crossover. Not in a collision but a sensitive rising in awareness of another force. The short staccato E (ey) begins to establish boundaries, moments of holding the outward flow at bay introducing possibilities for something new to be created. Becoming aware, creating a consideration for the new or other, sensitivity to what is in the backspace, and establishing a duality are all part of this energy. Like a pendulum, the direction of flow is arrested after the first exuberant extension.

Including this vowel E (ey) *awakens* the human being to action or defense. Crossing the limbs in front of the body is a defensive act toward what comes toward us from the periphery.

A counter movement now is introduced and the two opposite forces meet while the sound E (ey) is heard. The being of E (ey) with swift lightness, raised arms crossed over, warding off the overwhelming flow of forward movement. NAY—no further, stop! In nature we find the same gesture when a rapidly flowing stream is interrupted by a stone or tree branch. The turbulence creates small vortexes; a circular dynamic becomes the origin for a new impulse.

In the recognition of a threefold human being (body, soul, and spirit), it follows that the creation takes place in the beginning of things (Genesis). The soul as an organ housed in the physical body, finds its origin through Gaya undergoing a descent into darkness.

Plate 49: Eurythmy gesture of E

In the sounding of A (ah) throughout space a new impulse arises. It is the E (ey) sound, thwarting the unobstructed forward flowing impulse of beginnings. It becomes the place for examining the incarnating process.

First the human being, **The One**, imbued with spirit, descends from the outer reaches of the celestial spheres with a relationship to the Gaya, who as God-Creator reaches out (over) from beyond other dimensions. Incarnating into the world of solidity by descending into the parental cells of reproduction, **The One** reveals threefold merging—father, mother, and cosmic visitor—introduced by the knowledge of embryogenesis. Two dynamics occur, one macrocosmic (the human spirit) coming from outer spaces, the other microcosmic (embryo) unfolding in the most intimate space of human anatomy, the pelvis; yet each has a similar reaction to the symphonic music of the spheres, the vowel sounds.

The vibrations of the distinct vowel sounds ring through the space. This journey can best be experienced within the body if the reader can evoke the imagination with the voice sounding the vowels as I have demonstrated. Taking ourselves through the vowel sounds (A E I O U) in bodily expression and pronunciation, one experiences a possibility of deeper penetration correlating with increased density. Ending with the U ("oo") sound, we experience a solid pillar, immovable, upright, and supporting, all contained within, sustainable and separate from Earth.

History of the Gnostic Myth

Throughout the ages, all the cultures of the East, West, South, and North had creative myths, a social foundation in which the gods descended, fructified the Earth, and left human beings to their own devices. Knowledge belonging to supra-earthly dimensions, the existence of creative gods, and the placement of the human being into the order of creation are all assigned to the spiritual aspect of humanity. We can find such stories in the ancient scriptures of Tibet, India, and Persia, and in the Talmud and Gnostic books of the Jewish people. The inheritance of this material is vouchsafed to all human beings regardless of their orientation and will be a source for the recognition of the power of **The One**. It becomes clear that human beings are the only spiritual entities to pursue a path into matter. The gaze of multiple Gods follows us with the creator god Gaya leading us down into ever increasing density. We experience this imaginative picture as a powerful reminder that loneliness will be felt if the "I" is cut off from the reality of existing gods. These beings do have a vital interest in human individuality.

Out of this Gnostic myth, with Gaya as the mother to lead humanity toward new existence, an electrifying story unfolds. Her descent from the Godhead is not in silence but, with the background of the music of the spheres, the cosmic ringing of the vowels, with all creative forces influencing the process of becoming. It is not given to humanity to abide by; it becomes a subjective imagination that can fit in each human being's personal confession of faith (The Credo).

Humans, as created light beings, are assigned a place in creation as the tenth hierarchy. Humans are described as descending into the dark cold prison of solidity created by Gaya. In the struggle for release and return to the Father God, humans are assigned to generate Love and Freedom as an investment for the entire created world. In this process of evolution, creative sound, experienced as a vibrational music or word, influences the travelers. The sounding of the vowels will continue to be an experience in the process of solidification.

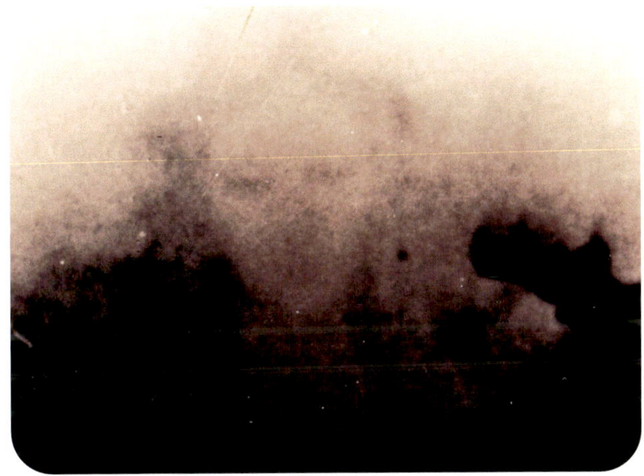

Plate 50: Image of Sophia (detail of Plate 26, page 26)

It can also be imagined that this Gaya being, in her descent, escorts and protects the human sparks in their becoming. An imagination of how the step-wise birth of the soul occurs, we can find in the powerful myth of Gaya, also known to us as the Sophia, relating to the planetary bodies (solar system). She created the Earth and remains on the level of our existence as a pure refined presence still incorporated in all of living matter. Although some of humanity remains unaware, **SHE IS WITH AND IN US**. In her evolution she is born anew as unsoiled human nature. She can be seen in suprasensory experiences of pure souls such as children. She will communicate with those human beings whose childlike existence can endure her presence. Goethe, in *Faust,* names her the Eternal Feminine redeeming the fallen human being.

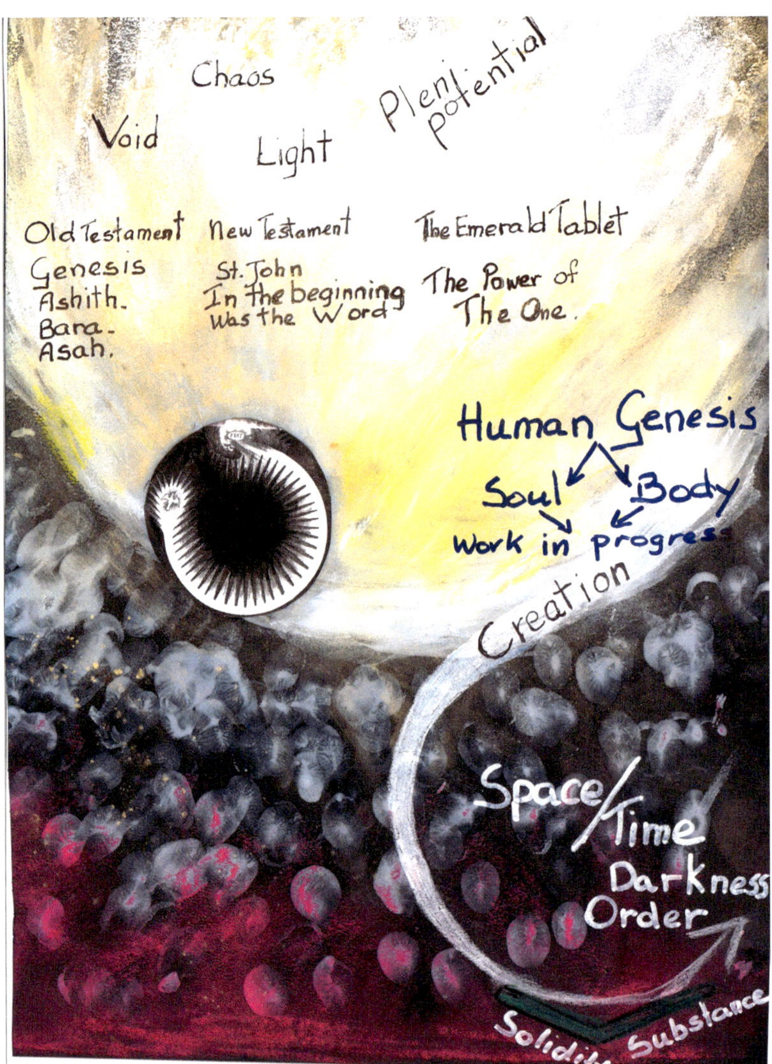

Plate 51: Soul genesis

The presence on Earth of millions of individualities, reflecting their uniqueness in the protein scaffolding they carry, is in itself a wondrous cosmic occurrence to be contemplated. The individuality, introduced as **The One,** through the work in the Emerald Tablet, has an intimate relationship to this feminine celestial being.

We will consider the creative process one witnesses in the evolution and maturation of the human soul and physicality. Imagination enables us to share in the Gnostic creation myth of Gaya, who is identified here as the "SOUL of HUMAN"

This is the pluripotent moment of Gaya setting out from the heavens. The Bible (Gen. 1:2) describes the darkness, referring to an immaterial existence as void and chaos. This nothingness referred to in the Hebrew original text was without time or space. It could be recognized in a condition of pure intense light. It held many possibilities, chaos seethed, new potentials were constantly emerging. Divine beings worked as one, they obeyed the rules of a grand being referred to as *THE FATHER GOD*. IT existed as radiation of pure love. Through ITS presence all was made possible. Without ITS presence nothing was made. Humanity was the latest creation, behind the nine hierarchies already ruling and working throughout the heavens as creators of worlds.

The building of the physical body is relegated to **The One** and becomes the story of embryogenesis. Dimensions of time and space are the accouterments of the earthly physicality dived into by **The One** at the moment of merger in the act of fertilization.

I give to you the beautiful myth of the Gaya (*Gaia*), Sophia captured in a poem by an Estonian woman, her Mother God stepping from the highest and loftiest abode and dwelling after the fiat is consented to by the Father God. When pure light meets darkness or absence of light, red is created.

On foot
I had to walk through the solar systems,
before I found the first thread of my red dress.
Already I sense myself.
Somewhere in space hangs my heart,
sparks fly from it, shaking the air,
to other reckless hearts.

—Edith Södergran (1892–1923)

Soul Genesis

To understand the existence of a soul, a personality, and an individuality dwelling within the same earthly body makes us question our own uniqueness and signature. What is the story of my beginning? Can the manifestation of the personality, changing with different incarnations, make a claim in developing sense and soul organs with renewed improvement? In the last greeting of a dying Cherokee, the inculcated wish for *a better life the next time* is expressed.

Plate 52: NASA nebula

First one must acknowledge that the Sophia escorts and protects **The One** from the state of A (ah). **The One** experiences safe passage through the celestial spheres, ending with incarnation in form—the process of conception. At this crossing, the stream of the A (ah) becomes turbulent and fluctuating, finally breaking down into individual drops cut off from the stream. Whereas the A (ah) is timeless, the introduction of flowing time is a result of this drop formation. On Earth the individual exists in time.

The human "I," or soul, experience is steeped in time. Memories are the cornerstone of the soul experience. We gather the sensory perceptions of a lifetime granted to us through the natural world—this world being our Earth, so beautifully organized and maintained by the Mother Sophia.

The human's organ of soul comes under the purview of our cosmic mother (referred to as *maya* by Rudolf Steiner), and the poignant meditation in the Misraim service reminds all of **The Ones** that she will continue to present herself through the HUMAN SOUL.

Each human spark created received an assignment: "As individualities they would descend into the darkness, and become the first hierarchy creating and subsequently penetrating solid substance" (Myth of Creation). Solid substance means the world of molecules. This dense material is to serve as the garment of **The One**, becoming home to the human being and reenacted until free from the wheel of repetitive life karma. Bondage and darkness is assigned to humanity, stimulating the desire for freedom and light. Humanity, as the tenth hierarchy, was given the task to develop a soul disposition toward LOVE and FREEDOM. This would be an original contribution to benefit all of creation.

> If you approach me with true desire for knowledge
> I shall be with you.
> I am the germ and the source of your visible world,
> I am the sum of the light in which your soul lives,
> I am she who rules in space,
> I am she who creates the cycles of time,
> Fire, Air, Light, Water and Earth obey me.
> Perceive me as the immaterial origin of all matter.
>
> And as I have no husband on Earth, call me therefore "Maya."
>
> —Rudolf Steiner, *Freemasonry and Ritual Work* (p. 244)

Through the descent of the divine Gaya, humanity became endowed with the sense organs, a soul, and the "I" organization, three distinct aspects in the conscious human being. Sophia, the divine being who accompanies us on our descending journey into darkness, bestows upon human beings these three aspects—the soul in its capacity to Love and Hate; the sense organs, of which only five are familiar to us at this time; and the "I"-organization, also identified as the Self, who observes conscious activity and inserts the processes of thinking, feeling, and will.

Let us again repeat the journey of the Gaya and find the correlation between the soul and the physical body of **The One** in the following lines. With the A(ah) resounding, space opens, and Gaya, clothed in a luminous white garment, steps out of the world of Heaven. Millions of light sparks (human spirits) follow her passionate descent, awaiting birthing into dark realms. While hearing the A(ah) throughout cosmic space, the light meets dark, creating the color red. Gaya's garment flows in waves and frills like the Aurora high over the poles, high above the atmosphere, undulating. *So far! So close!*

Overwhelmed with magnificence and familiarity, humans, as sublime light sparks, sense and wait. The first acquisition in this birthing process is what is sensed by Gaya—the color of red. This is the awakening of the soul through sense. A stage in consciousness is where the human "I" lives in its newly achieved sense perception of color and sound. The "I" embodies sense perception as the first step in creation. The gesture is one of overflowing, perpetual motion, tumbling into dark, creating red in its wake. The human "I" dives into existence, and red blood will become its organ. This becomes the imprint for the "I" (our individuality) and might also be referred to as destiny.

In our creation myth, Gaya is freed from her exsanguination. She adjusts, and human soul is freed from bondage to only the senses of vision and hearing.

Evolution of the Soul-Psyche

In the imaginary breathing-out ("I" am not) followed by breathing in ("I" am), we discover the reality of imprisonment within the boundaries of a physical existence. Spirit freedom is sacrificed when polarities, with the choices they offer, are introduced in bodily formation. The soul receives within its boundary the duality of Love/Hate, the capacity for desire or rejection. The bodily development (embryogenesis) creates boundaries to which the Soul adheres.

In the embryo, the sequence of development is first the formation of red blood cells, capillaries of the periphery, smaller and larger venous system, large veins, the heart. This duct system is assigned to contain the organ of blood, the seat of the "I." **The One** has found its place from which to rule the embryogenetic development. This circulatory organ becomes responsible for the delivery of the blood throughout the physical body. The heart itself functions as a sense organ, interrupting the flow of blood and listening to information from both the upper and lower poles of the body. The blood, as an organ of fluid, is recognized as the bearer of the most sacred aspect of the human being—the "I," the human soul. Its expression is through the rhythm of the pulsing heart with respiration, the contraction and relaxation of peripheral capillaries of the skin. The autonomous nervous system becomes the servant, as when we blush or pale in soulful meeting with "the other."

There are two illustrations of the Child Artist I want to bring to your attention. One is the heart (plate 53, page 73), a fragment of plate 3, the other is the Sun (plate 22, page 20), from plate 21. Of interest is what we can extract from enlarged representations. The heart, drawn with four colors, shows a yellow winged being in the center. In the Sun picture, we notice a window with a distinct face looking down upon the scenario of the Three Kings. The heart, ruled by the Sun, plays a prominent role in the evolution of a human being. We can ask a child, "Where is your soul?" The child will place a hand on the left side of the chest, where the heart pulsates.

Physical Incarnation—Soma

The human "I" bathes in the red color, the color of Gaya's garment.

This becomes the color of the human blood formed in the embryo.

Blood cells move from the periphery toward the center (centripetal).

The "I"-organization claims the blood-cell formation, and with a rhythmic pendulum movement establishes the circulation.

In the Embryo, a new stage is entered.

Fluid flowing from the periphery into the center, centripetal coming abruptly to rest at the center.

This becomes a place where mingling of air and liquid is possible.

A new creative possibility is added, that of foam formation.

Fluid penetrated with air makes bubbles, like the interruption of liquid flow creating foam. Formation of alveoli in the lung and the globules in the glandular organs are an outcome of this dynamic process.

The lung organ makes it possible for the "I"-organization to experience the pulsing and rhythm at the point where streaming blood and potential flow of air intertwine.

Through the awareness of the space-behind created in the sound E(ey), the first organ is created—the heart.

The embryonic task, under the vowel sounding, is completed when a crossover between two tubular structures, later designated as venous and arterial streaming, takes place. The heart becomes a hollow space.

The two organs in the chest region, heart and lung, become the organs that express feeling. The soul experiences feeling through pulses and rhythms—the intersecting flow of blood with flowing air.

In the imagination of Eastern medicine, the heart function is described in the following meditation.

> It governs the blood
> It controls the blood vessels
> It manifests in the completion
> It houses the Shen
> It opens the tongue
> It controls the sweat

Here, one may appropriately ask: "Is the heart a pump?" Independence of soul is established once the developing embryonic organ can imbibe light and warmth. Once the individuation takes place the interior space fills with blood (the seat of the soul), establishing a rapid and expansive growth pattern of tissue. **The One's** incarnation phenomenon becomes the individuation process resulting in a sole identity. Once in a state of mature adulthood, the strength of blood assists in the struggle for a virtuous existence. **The One** has been tasked for its incarnation on Earth and is able to express the self through both the soul and the physical body. The personification of **The One** on Earth observes, corrects, encourages, tutors, and loves the earthly counterpart with utmost endurance and patience. The "I" is present in the expression of the faculties in both body and soul, with which all humans are endowed. Foremost, while dwelling on Earth, a strong "I" expresses the soul qualities of balance between the capacities of focused thinking, feelings as expressed in emotions, and control of the will. Also recognizable are physical expression, endurance, and perseverance throughout physical hardships or failures.

Plate 53: Heart

Gaya created for humanity a solar system of planetary bodies in which the Sun becomes the pivotal life-imbuing central sphere (star). Earth has soul, created as the habitat for life, becomes the body of the Gaya, whom we identify as he living entity Sophia. Through Her creative impact, the human body constitutes forces from all the planets, thus providing its organization (astral body). The eternal feminine represents humanity in its wholeness. It is the Sophia intertwined with the human being (*Anthropo-Sophia*), whose wisdom culminates in the highest spiritual aspect—the wondrous physical living body. It can be called "The Symphony of the Created World."

Embryogenesis: Incarnation of The One

As a field of science, embryology allows us to examine the day-to-day incarnation process of the individual human being. It represents the union of two reproductive cells during fertilization and its development. It does not include the incarnation of the human spiritual spark at the moment of the cellular merger. Through the work of the Child Artist, our consciousness of this process is awakened. Our interpretation of the Child Artist's drawings becomes an essential part in considering the formative force of **The One**.

Natural science teaches that the dynamic of the male and female reproductive cells is represented simply as a merger of two cells becoming one. However, a new story of incarnating human beings can unfold and be contemplated by introducing a new possibility, derived from the combined works of the Child Artist, the gnostic myth of Gaya (bringing humanity into the fulfillment of incarnating "in the flesh"), and teachings of the highly respected initiate of Alchemy, Hermes Trismegistus, and his *Tabula Smaragdina*, or Emerald Tablet.

Still, in the dynamic flow of the Ah, the sojourn of the Spirit from the higher regions is completed. It needs to be acknowledged that the element of time is negligible, because the genesis aspect is beyond the dimensions of time.

Plate 54: Cosmic sled on choppy waters (revisited)

The descent of **The One** from cosmic regions is eloquently presented in three pictures by the Child Artist. They represent a journey in space between Sun and Earth. In the first picture (plate 12 page 12), the origin of **The One** is suggested when the artist includes the Sun in the upper left corner. The Sun and Moon, represented as the fountain symbol, become the sustainable sources of warmth, light, and life that the existence on Earth will incorporate. The "ship" available to him is fitted out with a perfect round cosmic sail, and an intricate rudder system. The cabin is closed designating the cosmic being as a passive passenger. A chaotic plasmatic presence is situated on the front bow.

A very different impression is created with the illustration titled "Cosmic sled..." (above). Studying this glorious representation, we are drawn into the downward movement of the vehicle, with choppy waves beneath and the masterful command by which the captain pilots from far above. The seat is elevated like a throne, the rudder is solidly connected to all the limbs, and for The One there is only one way to go...onward! The steering mechanism is again an important part of the drawing and it tells us a story of unwavering intentionality.

Plate 55: The Guardian (detail)

Moments before penetration into solidity at the moment of fertilization, **The One** reflects the uncertainty experienced (a preview). The enormity of the earthly task, facing loneliness, deprived of spirit sensing, would all be overwhelming if not for the angelic guardian standing right next to the small figure, embracing the traveler with a long arm of protection (plate 55, from plate 14, page 13).

Now the sail becomes like angel wings as a reminder that return is still possible? Around the incarnating being, earthly life forces find expression in multiple birds flying around the boat. The heart-shaped structures represent symbolically **The One's** capacity for love toward all that will be encountered. There is a disconnection (headphones?) to the always-available cosmic musical succor. During the meeting on the horizontal plane, a guardian or guide accompanies the enthusiastic traveler.

Plate 56: Contributions of three beings

These interpretations of the symbolic illustrations are subjective, and imaginative freedom is practiced owing to our limitations in grasping the suprasensory. Whether to name the incarnating **One** *Spirit* or *individuality* is irrelevant. The process of incarnation is recognized in this definition.

> Incarnation is the descent of a sentient being from outer cosmic regions. During the merger or material manifestation of this force, whose original nature is immaterial, the conception or birth is completed. (Wikipedia)

Incarnation and conception occur under an evolutionary dynamic in the sound of the E ("ey"). New beginnings are created during and after the dynamic of two streams crossing. The dimension of time, foreign to spirit, is introduced. The male and female gametes are prepared long before the fertilization to be haploid in chromosomes. The splitting of chromosomes from the natural number of forty-six to only twenty-three in both gametes is a necessary precursory step to the fertilization process. Of note is the amazing fact that each of these gametes contains unique protein configurations (snowflake).

This same gesture is observed in the spirit-being just before the sperm penetration of the ovum. While hovering over the parental gamete cells, a division into two streams or forces responsible for different activities in the development of the embryo is enacted. The first part, spirit-germ, connects with the physical body and is instrumental in determining form and shape. The second part, spirit-body, will individualize the embryo.

We can imagine that the spirit-germ chooses one particular sperm cell and directs that parental donor to penetrate the mother cell. Keep in mind that the male gamete determines gender. The incarnating human spirit uses the product of both the male and female gametes—the zygote. The blend of the content of both nuclei creates a condition of a multi-potential chaos. Out of this state, a unique human being is constituted. Genomes of both nuclei from the parental cells partake in combining spontaneously, directed by the spirit-germ. This seed, also called the morula, potentiates the shape and form for a new human being—*Homo sapiens*. An incarnating Spirit-being divides into two specific impulses playing a role in embryogenesis. The first split yielding the spirit-germ is "overseer" in the merger of male and female gamete and resulting cell cleavage, morula formation, and finally development of the blastocyst.

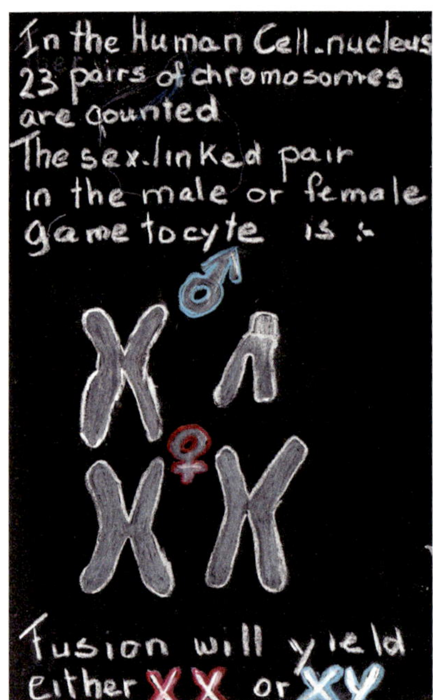

Plate 57: Gender chromosomes

With embedding, the blastocyst becomes trophoblast, nestling within the inner mucosa of the womb. Give or take twenty days, the final merger with the Spirit body is completed. Now we observe the formation of a threefold cell structure. From here on, specificity and the template of unique characteristics will develop.

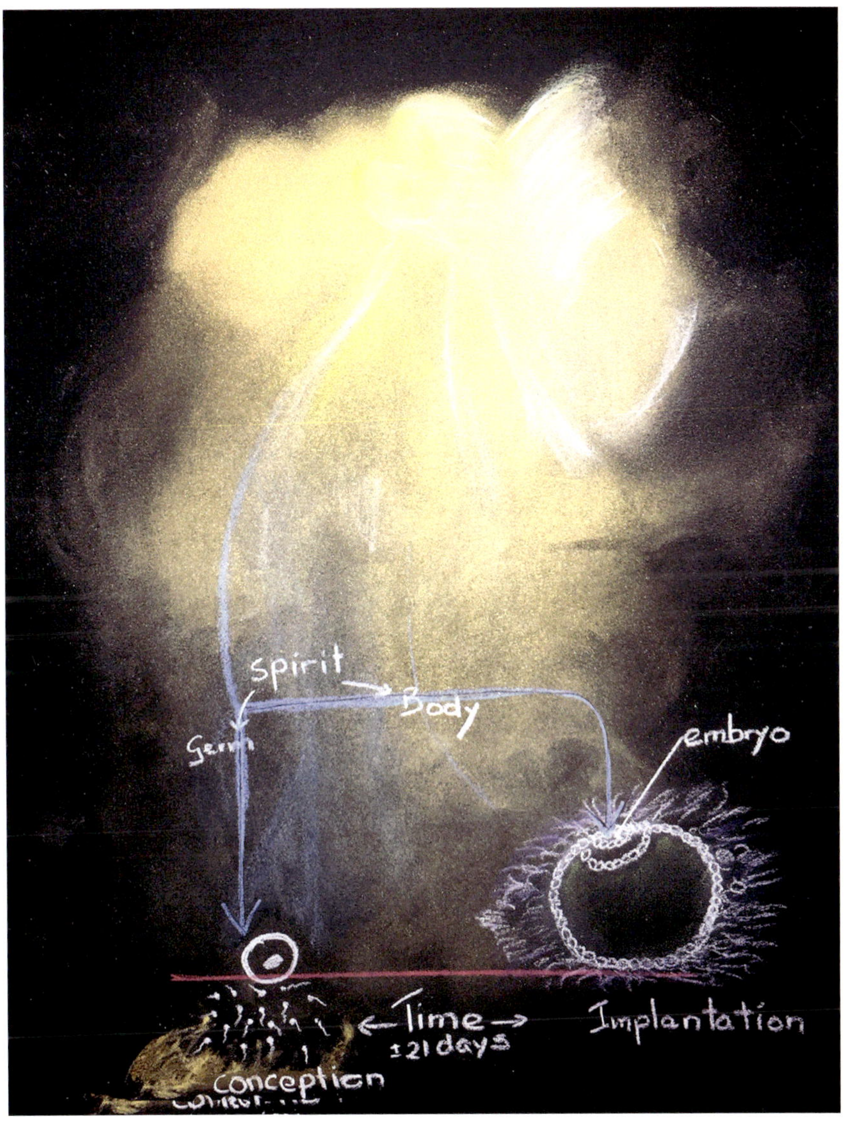

Plate 58: Incarnation of ***The One:*** *two activities and completion*

Polar opposites are introduced here. The dynamic sounding E ("ey") is partially instrumental in creating the condition of attraction between opposite gametes. Where the oocyte is exceptionally large, immobile, and filled with cytoplasm, the sperm cell is active, very mobile, and small, carrying only a concentrated nucleus with the twenty-three chromosomes. The gamete donated by the male parent must make a long and arduous journey to its final place of action.

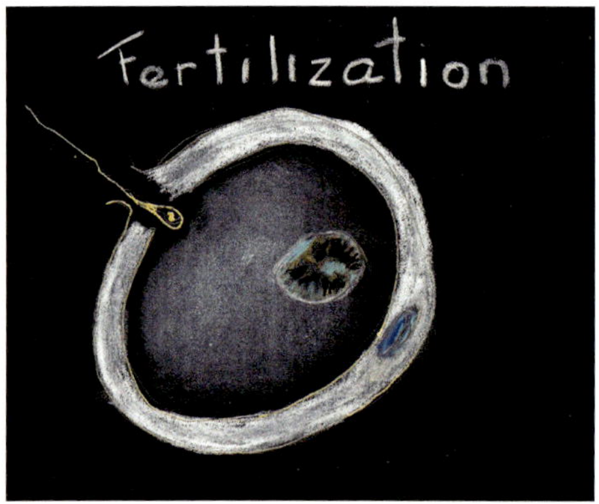

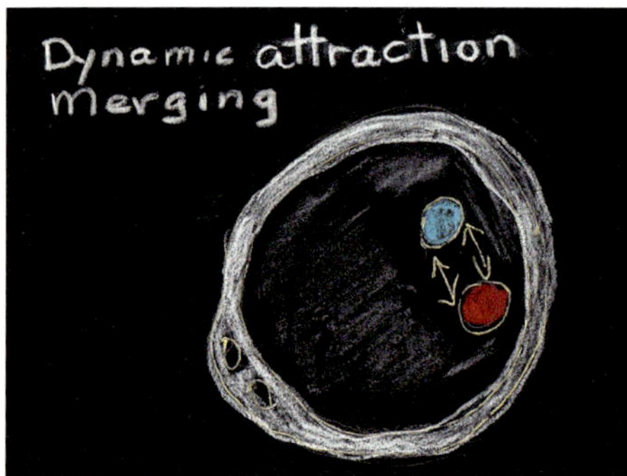

Plate 59 (above): Fertilization
Plate 60 (below): Dynamic attraction

The female gamete, the oocyte, is rich in cytoplasm, and provides an element of form. This pinhead-size egg cell bursts from the ovary during ovulation and is immediately surrounded by the soft tentacle-like protrusions of the fallopian tube (*fimbriae*). This is the place where these two opposite cell structures will meet for conception. The spirit being—sojourning in cosmic spaces and for us still foreign dimensions—undergoes a journey from above to below. This movement can be seen as crossing the threshold into material existence.

It can be imagined that the mother cell is tucked away in the inner recesses of the female pelvis, an area where negative pressure exists. The perfect round bowl presented as the female pelvic bone structure will spawn a vortex movement whereby the eye becomes a vacuum and asserts a negative pressure or suction on the content. This suction from below enables the sperm to swim deep into the womb, while from above the spirit-being awaits its merger (incarnation). We can have the imagination that the pelvis becomes like a

Grail made ready to receive a substance from beyond Earth.

We have to realize that the selection of a single sperm to penetrate the cell membrane of the oocyte, or "mother-cell," is not a haphazard occurrence that takes place as a random physiological process (fertilization). Penetration of the female gamete's membrane by the male gamete becomes a spiritual event. The germ cells are joined by the Spirit-germ. Embryogenesis asks for the cooperation of the most important entity in the process of fertilization, the incarnated Spirit-being, the newborn human entity—**The One**.

Let's move on to the second postulate of Hermes Trismegistus.

Plate 61: Buddha: above as below

Postulate II

> *The below is as the above, the above is as the below to perfect the wonders of* ***The One****.*

In its successful attempt to reach embodiment in the zygote, **The One** will claim domain of the parental cell. The phases of the first three weeks in the development from a one cell structure to a multi-cell, pea-size organism is studied in detail. The encapsulated nuclear zygote undergoes segmentation, or cell division, to reach a maximum of sixteen cells. The so-called morula can be compared to a plant seed, a cell bundle carrying identical, undifferentiated genetic material. This cell mass can be seen as "the wonder of **The One**." These embryonic stem cells can be harvested, processed, and donated as material for cloning (differentiated to organ or complete organism). In a state of metabolic suspension, possessing an autonomous biological development, each cell has the capacity to determine the physical development of an identical individual organism. This cluster of sixteen identical cells (*morula*) is the source for numerous scientific investigations, manipulations, and speculations. Not having been joined by the Spirit Body, it cannot claim individuality. It produces the stem cell used in regeneration of organ tissue. Cloning makes it possible that future identical humanoids could be produced in laboratories.

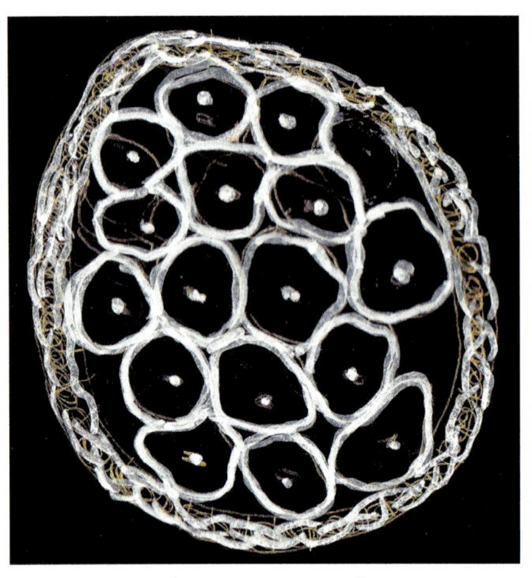

Plate 62: Morula

In Goethe's *Faust*, the Homunculus embodies the quest for pure spirit to be born into humankind, in sharp contrast to Faust's desire to shed his body and become pure spirit. For Paracelsus (*De natura rerum*, 1537), it is a little man who knows everything born from an alchemical procedure. Goethe's character Faust embodies the "little" man with full wisdom of the human being. The Homunculus, in its glass sphere (likened to the morula) contains the blueprint for human creation, although not inspirited. Could this allude to the *Philosopher's Stone* captivating the imagination of many researchers?

Of interest is the Child Artist's illustration (plate 66, p. 86), which places the seed on the left side. In his process of embryogenesis, a distinct humanoid figure is seen in the center. In this phase in embryogenesis, silence reigns, all metabolic activity ceases, and the Spirit-germ is suspended. The baton is raised. Creation is watching, breath held. This is the moment of autonomous biological development.

Once the morula is expelled from the confinement of the tube into the uterine cavity, the germinating power is quickened. Through cyst-making, a distinction arises between the cells that infiltrate and search for nutrients and the cells occupied with embryo-making that divide (Guus van der Bie, *Embryology*). After the blastocyst becomes part of the uterine wall, explosive expansion begins. The embryo (*trophocyst*) is nineteen days old and the spirit body, hovering over the genesis activity, now joins the development. Incarnation of the Spirit-being **The One** is complete and a new phase in the embryogenesis begins. No doubt the individuation process falls under the vowel sound "I" (ee); however it becomes a vital part of the story that now unfolds.

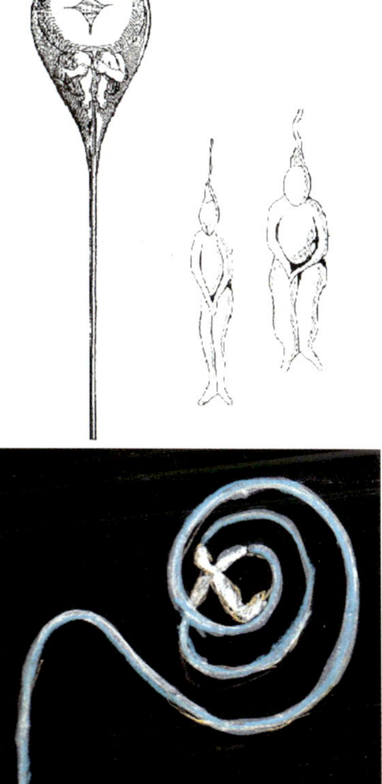

Plate 63: Depictions of the homunculus

At the moment the spirit body joins the expanding, developing cell structure, completing the incarnation of **The One,** a germ-disc is recognizable in the inner cell mass. It is remarkable that the cells of these three layers each have a designated function connected to bodily development. We have discussed to the threefold constitution of the physical body. In the embryo we see that the foundation for this constitution is organized as early as the third week, especially where different cell constructions assume responsibility for organ formation. Just as music incites a dancer or a ball activates a game, similarly, through the dynamic activity inherent in growth movements of the three layers, ectoderm, mesoderm, and endoderm, the threefold organization in the embryonic organism, is established. These layers each lend an orderly development with its respective functions in the embryo. The ectoderm, mesoderm, and endoderm layers each contain cells that execute a specific task. The large orchestra made available to **The One** has a gloriously perfect conductor. The cells of each layer become instruments that are directed by forces from "above." In the process of invagination, these layers begin to fold, embrace, polarize, and find a designation for their unique role in the development of the embryo. Surrounded by fluid on both sides, the mass now graduates to an embryonic disc and the distinct three layering.

For instance, the cells of the ectoderm will be responsible for the development of the skin epidermis, the neurons of the central nervous system, and pigment cells. The cells of the mesoderm layer are given the task of muscle cell development (heart, uterine, skeletal, and smooth muscle) and red blood cell formation. The endoderm layer contains cells that will be available for the formation of the lung, the liver, the endocrine organs of thyroid and pancreas, and the epithelial cells of all organs. Contemplating the hidden value of threefolding, we meet the evolutionary separation in the soul life forces of

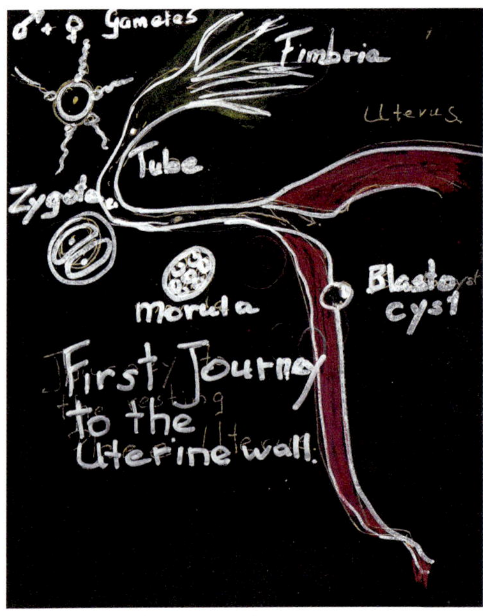

Plate 64: The journey

thinking, feeling, and activity of will. Thinking with the "head" assigns the mind as the brain in action. The expression "touching" is often used when an emotion stirs us. Stimulating the sense organ of touch evokes strong feelings. The numerous red blood cells in the skin find their origin in the mesoderm. The cells of the endoderm layer become responsible for excretion, purification, and nutrition.

The One becomes the conductor in a symphony of creating the physical body. Knowing cosmic wisdom from the vertical in-streaming governs the execution of the formation process. Music from the heavenly spheres, as interpreted through the vowel sounds, guides the formation of all the organs, step by step.

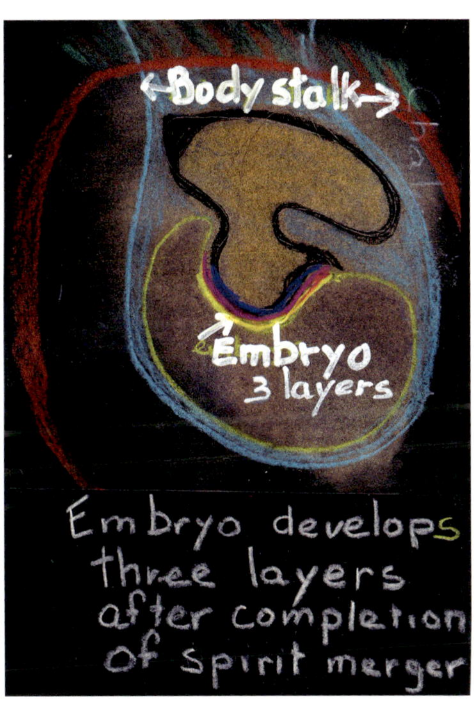

Plate 65: Body stalk carrying three layers

The creation of the physical body, after all, becomes an individual task, a mandate from **The One**, with familiarity of this outward flow of cosmic knowing as witnessed in the illustrations of the Child Artist.

Let us examine the middle section of the template drawing titled "Embryogenesis" (plate 66, next page). First, a somewhat transparent helmet arises from the right side, representing symbolically the consolidated mineral earth. This dome, with five individual colored hair-like appendages in the front, could be interpreted as an artistic presentation of the central nervous system. The five sense organs that develop first belong to the eye, ear, nose, tongue, and skin. The fact that this system functions in a silica-rich environment is illustrated by the artist's connection to the Earth's crust, which is composed ninety percent of silicate minerals.

The center area, drawn in red and orange, occupies a substantial space in the embryonic development. What is obvious is the interpenetration of two structures in a tentacle-like fashion (formation of somites?). If the dome and red-colored cell mass represent the ectoderm, it is the union between the ectoderm and the mesoderm (orange) that becomes information represented symbolically by the Child Artist. Indeed, there is a process of enclosing the cells of the ectoderm by the mesoderm cells. This structure eventually carries the spinal chord embedded in the vertebra.

Plate 66: "Embryogenesis," the Child Artist's embryo

The artist colors the third layer and its voluminous organ in blue surrounded by a cystic lake. This part of the embryo is connected firmly to the Earth. Five suction cups reach out from the central mass into a vesicle below. The cells of the endoderm layer assume the functions of nutrition, metabolism, and excretion. The heavy mass surrounded by water resembles the liver, representing the largest metabolic organ in the embryo. Of all embryonic organs, the liver functions at the optimum level with a very low blood oxygen saturation. The dark-blue color is well chosen.

Scientifically obtained dissections of numerous human embryos augmented the study of embryology with accurate information. All students can familiarize themselves with the dynamic process of cell separation and the specific function of cell clusters. The developing embryonic tissue exhibiting sophisticated early displays in the designation of three layers is correlated with the earthly incarnation of the Spirit-body.

Comparing the drawings of our six-year-old Child Artist to the gleaned accurate microscopic information informs us about the suprasensory process. Unraveling these riddles helps us realize that knowledge of intricate processes is carried as memories to newborns assigned to create their own body. After incarnation, **The One** becomes the conductor. The baton is raised, in focused expectation, waiting the right moment to lead the orchestra into a symphony of their own creation. What is brought by the individuality, **The One**, onto the earthly plane? Incarnation as well as reincarnation is an acceptable philosophy. Memories from the past are brought by **The One** and stored in the etheric body, the body fluids that surround the embryo. Spiritual content is stored during the time of development in utero. The young Child Artist brings us hidden memories of learning beyond adult understanding.

Postulate III

> *And as all things come from* ***The One****, from the meditation of* ***The One****, so all things are born from* ***The One****, by adaptation.*

Full authority is given to **The One** in the third postulate of the Emerald Tablet. Hermes Trismegistus inaugurates the process of **The One** completing incarnation. Full power is bestowed to **The One,** who can oversee the development of its own body. Authenticity is established only after the chaos created in the first process of chromosomal blending has been attained. Order out of chaos in the parental nucleus means adaptation.

What is the relationship to the Mother at this stage of development? The embryo occupies a space no larger than one to two centimeters, has its own genetic signature foreign to the host, and no exchange of blood is found. The nutrition of the embryo is secured by the nutrient osmosis in the cell vacuities present in the uterine wall. The embryo is a "parasite," although it is certainly not rejected but embraced by the mother. Could it be that the integration of the human being, with its fourfold activity of warmth, light, living water, and chemical exchange, procures a foundation for acceptance by the mother? The blissful nature of the expecting mother is not surprising. New life is a gift. Let us proceed to the fourth postulate.

Postulate IV

> *Its father is the Sun, its mother Is the Moon;*
> *the Wind carries it in its belly, its nurse is the Earth.*

With this postulate, Hermes Trismegistus introduces us to the four Aristotelian elements—fire, air, water, and earth—which deserve attention regarding the constitution of **The One**. The four-body concept was first discussed as a foundation stone in Anthroposophy. The sources of the four elements used for contemplating the fourth postulate of the Emerald Tablet are rich and meaningful. Keep in mind that the total postulate was given to the students of Alchemy involved with their own purification and spiritual growth. Repetitive study of the content would move the soul-life into the desired state of openness and understanding.

The cadaver is a presentation of only the mineral chemistry, referred to as "dust," or salt of the earth. Functioning as a living entity requires animation arising from the infusion of living water, the circulation of air and penetration of fire providing warmth. Life is provided to **The One** by the parental gametes of opposing forces. The physiognomy of the male gamete is small and mobile, as if stirred by centrifugal forces of the radiating warmth and air. The female gamete moves sluggishly; the cell is filled with living water in which the chemical exchanges dominate. **The One** penetrates the gametes to acquire substance (earth as nurse), and with three other aspects enables completion of the fourfold etheric body. Father Sun donating the aspect of warmth/fire and Mother Moon donating living water and Wind as carrier of the air in the belly.

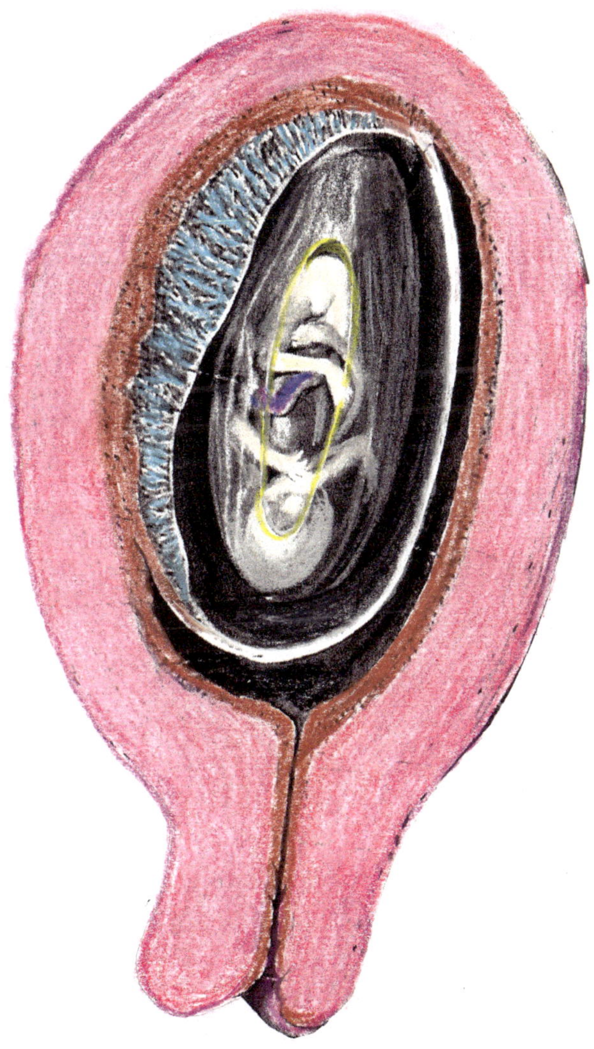

Plate 67: Embryonic developed fetus tucked in womb

Throughout the first weeks of pregnancy, **The One's** contortions can be compared to a balloon dancing in the air. Opposing currents give rise to a three-dimensional dynamics that ultimately end with the well-known tucked-in, flexed, fetal presentation at the end of three months.

The image of the embryonal urge for cell growth—differentiating into zones and dividing into distinct functions with responsive placement into opposite poles that cannot unfold in an orderly way unless pressure from the outside continues—places the observer in the midst of a moving marvel of wonders. A memory of the sequence of these movements will enrich our own imaginative powers, which is of vital importance for the future.

It stands to reason that the new incarnation (a spiritualized embryonic body) can evoke a bird's-eye view and uses the directing forces that streams in from cosmic spaces as music from the spheres, using the suprasensory organs still available. Examples of these forces were demonstrated in the Chladny figures (1835).

Plate 68: Vowels in air

Here, I want to introduce the body of work by a well-known physician and student of Anthroposophy, Hans Jenny (*Cymatics*). His experiments, which demonstrate the effects of sound vibrations on solid surfaces, were painstakingly photographed for posterity. This body of work can be seen as groundbreaking as illustrations of formative forces. His insight into the problems of modern physiology and biology spurred the experimental field to include the effects of vibrations in concrete medium. This experimental phenomenology was called *cymatics*.

Johanna Zinke, a student of Rudolf Steiner, also conducted independent research using smoke to develop creative vowel patterns from speech. Her work renforces the creative shaping of matter through tonal resonance in the human head.

These illustrations exemplify the possible effects that vibrations can effect on a medium. The shape, density, size, and form are all dependent on the material being excited, its shape and form, as well as the highlighting material (sand, smoke, dye), and the sound frequencies to which it is exposed. The spiritualized primitive embryonic body (**The One**) finds itself in a self-regulating domain.

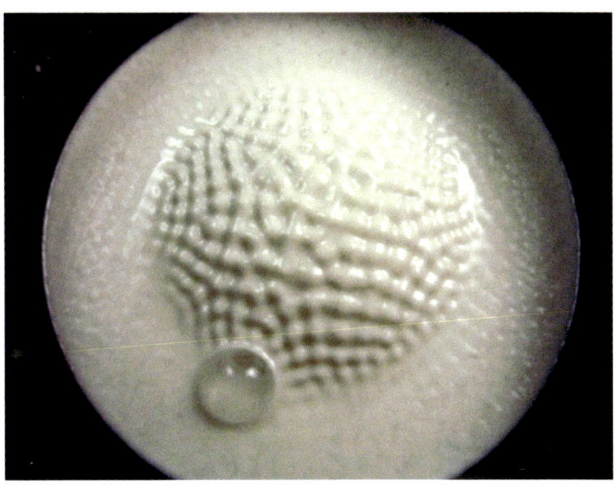

Plate 69: Cymatics in fluid: Cornstarch and water solution and sine wave vibration

Embryogenesis is experienced as a journey through the ***kingdoms of the Earth***. The male and female gamete just before their demise (i.e., if fusion would not occur) are doomed to die. This fact introduces us to the mineral world. Being on the verge of not being enlivened is a near-death experience. After this, we witness a seed existence, the morula, followed by an image of rapid growth, much like we see, for instance, in a mushroom and other images of the plant world. The process of invagination to form gastrula, or pocket, belongs to the development of a member in the animal kingdom.

The body of the embryo is animalized as soon as the spirit germ and spirit body merge as one to become whole as the spiritual entity in the embryo of **The One**.

In natural science, ontogeny describes the history of the development of an individual. In the animal kingdom it pertains to the developmental history of an organism within its own lifespan, as distinct from phylogeny, which refers to the evolutionary history of the species. Darwinism underscores ontogeny, the human species evolving up the rungs of the animal kingdom ladder through adaptation.

However, the argument that the phases in phylogeny have ceased after the human species entered evolution has validity. Suddenly, all the species of the animal kingdom can be seen as stepping stones toward the ultimate goal of the Earth becoming the habitat for humanity (*Homo sapiens*). In the phylogeny of the human embryo we find phases when the biological stages are reenacted, such as plant seed, fungoid imitation, early amphibian life, and zoological representations toward the higher mammals, ending early in the embryogenetic process when the distinct features for the upright human declares itself. The gestalt of uprightness distinguishes the human from the "apeman." The volume of cranial content enables the human to connect with an all-encompassing wisdom of which little is understood today. But it is the heart that will become the center of all human efforts. This challenging statement becomes a new imagination, underwriting thinking in the vertical dimension. Surely the Child Artist has made us aware of the wonders in the heart with his drawing (plate 3, page 4).

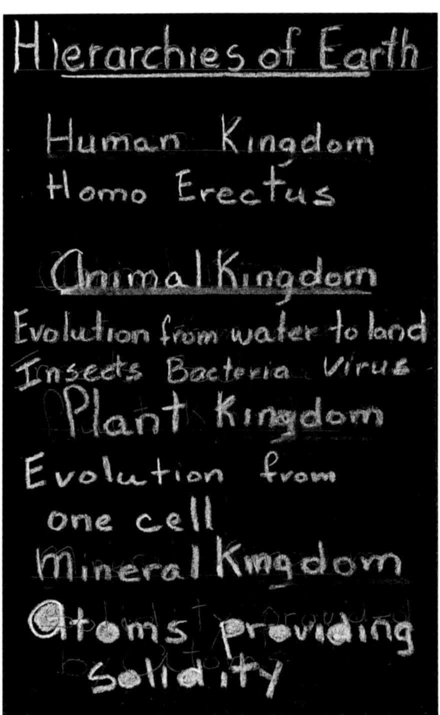

Plate 70: Hierarchies of Earth

It is recognized that the fetal tissue remains surrounded and continues to produces an environment containing exceptionally high silicon content. One wonders about the reason for such an aberrance, unless it is used by **The One** to strengthen the senses (hear the Music of the Spheres). One can imagine that the high silicon content of the tissue enhances the transmission of suprasensory messages from the cosmos. The embryonic tissue becomes an "antenna."

Awed by the rapid turn of events in the first few weeks of embryonic development, Hermes Trismegistus describes the process in his fifth postulate.

Postulate V

> *It is the Father of all wonders of the whole world,*
> *Its power is perfect, when it is transformed into Earth.*

The role of father in a culture of three thousand years ago (when these postulates appeared) was bestowed on a protective leader, usually a person or deity who was supreme (half god, half human), worthy in the role of a god who had full understanding of the life processes in the world it inhabited, performed miracles, and received adoration from this world. In this postulate, "It" is assigned the role of "Father." **The One** is named the originator of the wonders that **The One** himself performs in the process of incarnating. The adoring exclamation over this postulate, praising the power of perfection in the task of incarnating, is not lost on the reader. Adoration is deserved, because the wonders performed in the process of transformation from the Spirit incarnation into the human body are sublime.

Could embryogenesis, as performed by **The One,** be praised because it announces a new step in the evolution of Earth and the human being? Not only "its" ability to incarnate is praised, but also the explicit potential of **The One** to create a human body in its perfection as the culmination in Creation. Connecting the "whole world" with the appearance of the human on Earth could give Genesis, as written by Moses, an unexpected twist. The Sophia, present in the human soul, created the sphere of the Earth for the human being to inhabit a physical, solid body. Spiritual Science assigns to the Earth three previous existences—ancient Saturn, ancient Sun, and ancient Moon, followed by the Earth (Steiner, *An Outline of Esoteric Science*). Each of these conditions led to the intensification of solid states. What was once warmth became light through air, then life in water, and, in the final stage, a hardened mineral solid mass, the world of molecules and chemistry on Earth. Humanity is witness to this creative process and recapitulates it in embryogenesis.

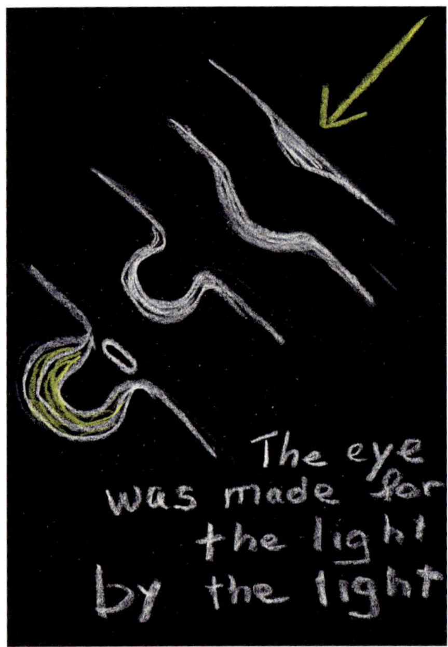

Plate 71: Process of invagination

This postulate confirms the recognition of power given to human beings as the center of creation. The two conscious individualities participating in this marvel and giving witness thereof have an understanding of Genesis and Embryo Genesis. Humanity recognizes these beings in the names of Moses and Hermes Trismegistus. The final destination for humanity is not a return to the heavens but a transformed Earth. The assignment is clear; only collective humanity can (and will) transform the Earth. How? The remaining postulates offer clear insights into future expectations.

At the moment of birth, a fetus emerges from water and becomes a land dweller with the need to breath in the airy atmosphere. The lung, used for the first time following birth, can be designated as the organ for living on Earth, the final step in the incarnating process of the individuality. Deployment of the alveolar pockets is an indication that the fetus has become an Earth citizen. As Goethe states, "The Eye is made by the light for the light." Thus, we can also reason that the breathing organ is made for *inspiration* by the spirit—**The One** (In-Spire). The One becomes a citizen of the Earth by partaking in the inhalation of the first gift of Earth, its atmosphere. Spirit becomes independently human with the first inspiration. At the other side of birth, the opposite process, the final breath at death, expiration, inaugurates a process of excarnation from the realm of Earth and birth, or a stepping into cosmic dimensions.

Birthing of the Child

In my forty years of practicing medicine in Columbia County, New York, the most exciting challenge was certainly to accompany the pregnant mother and assist her in the event of parturition. Usually it was the home birth desired by the parents, and as a practitioner of anthroposophic medicine in a rural area, I always considered it an honor to participate in a true learning process. Being a mother myself and giving birth in the mid-1960s in a sterile, cold hospital environment, I certainly had sympathies for the courageous woman who wanted to make a conscious choice to change the reception of the new earthling into an environment of warmth and joy.

In my personal history, I remember the battle to secure a natural birth and the right to breastfeed in a calculating medical system during the beginning of my path to motherhood. Even as a medical professional, it turned out that I was shunned, or rather left to my own devices, for all pre- and postpartum care—a bit of a nightmare. But then I had the strong memory of my own parents, both of whom as physicians had delivered women in their homes during the late thirties and the German occupation in northern Holland, which was not an easy time. Out of the hundreds of deliveries they assisted, there were no reported incidents of lost life for the mother, nor were there other complications caused by neglect. From them I sensed an all-pervading strength and levelheadedness and the capacity for allowing natural events for the mother to unfold. They had learned about patience, especially patience for the uterus to do its work, recognizing this muscle as an integral part of the birthing process.

Anatomically, the wall of the uterus has a dominant layer of smooth muscle fibers, both longitudinal and circular, which undergo a hypertrophy as well as an increase in the number of fibers up to twenty-four times during the ten lunar months of pregnancy. The female hormone estrogen stimulates the smooth muscle fibers to undergo hypertrophy and hyperplasia. The muscle fiber is unique in its response to hormonal messages. Contraction of the muscle can be stimulated by the hormone oxytocin, a pituitary gland extraction, and prostaglandins. This occurs naturally when the fetus' birth time has arrived and he/she is assigned the role as the captain of the ship named "Natural Childbirth." Contraction of those muscles allows expulsion of the content to take place not only through shortening of the body of muscles, but also by stretching the tight mouth or cervix so that the fetus can move down the birth canal and be delivered vaginally.

The growth of the fetus cannot be separated from the astounding development of the muscular mass of the uterine organ, which is not only the incubator for the fetus for ten lunar months, but will also become the tool of expelling the child during the birthing process. It is established that the tools for the child-controlled delivery are available in the form of hormonal secretion by the mother—oxytocin or the prostaglandins excreted by the fetal membranes.

Our understanding that each delivery is different and unique is absolutely valid when we consider that each birthed human being, **The One**, is a unique entity breathing the air of the Earth. For those of us who have assisted in births, this diverse experience is not a surprise. Our experience shows that a spontaneous relaxed birth is an expression of the being we assist into our midst.

How often have mothers remarked that there is a correlation between the child's first introduction to life on Earth (expression through birthing) and the signature of the new being in making fresh footprints on the Earth?

We notice the correlation between the progression of the natural birth and the nature and needs of **The One**. For instance, in children who know their wants, who are direct in their communications and are quickly satisfied, a delivery that was strong and short with no nonsense was experienced. Juxtaposed we have a birthing process that naturally unfolds more slowly, as if the child needs to take its time as an introduction for the parents to the true signature of this new being. A mother can experience both variations of the process at different births, indicating that the child must be heard during the process of birthing. Here the mother is given an opportunity to acquaint herself with the character or soul configuration of the child. The child's activity of dominating the uterine muscle contraction demonstrates the will forces, decisiveness, and eventual enthusiasm for life.

The work of the birth assistant becomes twofold. First one learns that natural childbirth can be divided into stages connected with the movement of the fetus into the birth canal. The completion of the first stage sets the second stage in motion, and so on. The assistant works with the parameters of time and progress established through knowledge and experience.

If it is accepted and understood that the child sets the pace, the assistant must serve two masters: the child and the mother. It is the mother who has to be convinced during the delivery that a part of her body does not belong to her. She must give it over to the incoming being so that the process of expulsion is enhanced. In this letting go, an enormous act of trust is established. Can I, as the woman in parturition, accept that the individual being, in the act of birthing, does not want to cause me pain? Does a natural process for cooperation exist? Yes!

As the uterine contractions become longer and more intense, a twilight zone can be entered, consciousness whereby the mother is able to concentrate on the prolongation of the individual contractions—relaxed trusting, an unconditional state of donating, and standing back to allow the child to take over. While assisting, we need to be present for the mother and father in a process of an unending sacrificial act.

An image that might help is the wordplay between *Hystera* and *Hysteria*. Both are Greek words. The root, *Hystera,* means Uterus. *Hyster-i-a* is a mental manifestation in which a second personality of emotional instability takes over. Hysteria could mean the state of losing it during parturition, the process of birth. Of course, hysteria is not only for the parents but also for the obstetric team. That is the time when modern intervention is being proposed. With the promise and belief that the modern medical system truly heals and does no harm, as consumers we trade in our rights and ability to self heal, along with the choice for dignified alternatives. There is no doubt in my mind that medical intervention may be justified even for obstetrical care. Witnessing the astounding rise of surgical intervention, promising the mother a pain-free, speedy, programmed delivery, the time has come for women to return to the drawing board and reconnect with what childbirth is really all about.

I have attempted to provide a new image from my own experience—an image that recognizes the triumph of natural childbirth for both the adult and the new Earth being. **The One** can find the intimacy and ecstasy of an experience that inspires the initiation of a parental unit. In the preparation for this portentous event we can use the following meditation throughout the pregnancy.

I stand before you
New miracle of life
You entered my being
And I await in awe
Your first footprint
In this your new life.

"Our children come through us; they are not of us"
KAHLIL GIBRAN, *The Prophet*

Sound I

The *I*, as a vowel, is easily identified as a gesture in which light streams down from the cosmos into the human being through an outstretched right arm, bathing and surrounding the human figure with a projection of independence and identity. An imagination of forces streaming out from Earth, penetrating the feet, legs and pelvis, straightening the posture in the upright position, is also familiar.

In the previous sections, illustrations and explanations were provided to introduce the incarnating process of **The One**. The historic reality of Alchemy and the collective memory thereof, the recognition of a creative process from the "Above" to the "Below," whether in the soul-spirit or physical embryogenesis, becomes source material during our contemplation in the "silent" time. Throughout the whole of creation the music of the spheres, resounding as the vibrational vowel sounds, accompanies the steps.

Birthing provides joy and the promise of possibilities. Contemplation of death provokes uncertainties and fears. One cannot help but recognize that evolution is the journey of **The One** throughout dimensions, a sojourn toward an ultimate goal. One might even be able to grasp the ultimate outcome in this glorious event; however, most of the time we get stuck on the plane of time and space when subjected to the mundane and personal crises, the daily "vale of tears."

This section centers on "I" fulfilling its task while breathing the Earth's air. The burden of the cloak of personality—the lack of insight into one's imperfections and the frustration of discovering that, despite years of outward gain, one's inner changes toward spirit knowledge have been largely elusive—must be examined while in the vibrational section of *"I."*

In my own biography, my role as a physician placed me in a position of trust and intimacy. In the role as obstetrician, the intimate birthing process was accompanied for at least one hundred deliveries. Many young people meet me now after twenty-five years, knowing that I was present during their first breath of life. This creates a mood of trust, a sense of continuity and availability in a field beleaguered by institutions. What is more intimate than the visit where the patient is facing his or her own aging and dying process? I do not turn away from extending myself, sharing with the patient an imagination of a birthing process in altered dimensions, a reality wherein a transformation instead of cessation can be enlivened by an image of a new birth.

Plate 73: Eurythmy gesture of I

The dying patient on chemotherapy pleads for help; it becomes impossible for those individuals to control the natural death process. They cannot consciously embrace the process of excarnation. They become witnesses to failure, severing the bond between the physical body and the life body. It is precisely the goal of pharmaceutical intervention to strengthen the attachment between these two bodies to obtain a longer life. The *quality* of life is not questioned. As the human "I" grows stronger, questions of immortality will emerge and need to be addressed, not only by the spiritual guide, but also by the healthcare worker in charge of the hospice situation. A patient's biography is examined as a series of stepping stones encountered by **The One** between cradle and grave. I also frequently use the autobiographical stories experienced throughout my life to illustrate the objective lawfulness of the Science of the Spirit also in my life.

The reality of space is a conscious experience for me. Through my eye I can see the light. Through my ear I can hear variations of tone. I can touch the solid objects and feel the quality of surfaces. My senses are the instruments used in soul awakening during social intercourse on the horizontal plane. Total silence in the outside world would equate to a cessation of all stimuli on the senses of the body. Overstimulation of one or two sense organs can cause distraction, preventing a growing child from discovering the inherent human potential in privacy without interference. Small children are unable to move and control their surroundings and are literally at the mercy of the sensitivity of the parents. Inner silence in adults is practiced during prayer or meditation.

Plate 74: Discover soul activity

Biographically, I was blessed with less distraction then usual, since both parents were professionals and, as a policy, left the baby mostly alone. A childcare nurse was our daily companion. I have no memory of my little sister; I do have visions of being sickly and having a cot next to my mother's bed. When awake, it was noticed that there was alertness to my surroundings, even curiosity for the activity around me. In an objective interpretation ever since birth, at the moment of one's first breath one can claim to have become an earthling with the capacity to use the senses, make percepts, and gather and store memories. To think my own thoughts and fashion concepts, unadulterated by influences from the outer world, was and remains my prerogative as **The One**.

Silence in which percepts and memories can be reevaluated is essential for the growing child to develop and recognize a sense for truth, beauty, and goodness. These are not inborn human qualities but acquired in the experience of a state of independence separate from the parental, hovering, doting, and often emotionally needy adult. Through the fleeting pain, fear, and threats, suffering is indeed experienced but resolved with the certainty of a reunion and always a safe home and parental succor.

Is it a requirement to be exposed to the pain of separation? In the silence of the suffering, many aspects of soul responses are developed and digested to become the tapestry of a rich emotional life. A child can learn the difference between what is on the outside and what is within, meeting duality in day consciousness. One role is that of the being of the child acting out with the desire to be noticed, with an assigned place in a family, pleasing and socializing. In other words, a child who learns the boundaries and limitations set up by the outside world also becomes aware that there are thoughts and feelings within—thoughts not shared with the outside world, private thoughts. What one thinks and feels becomes part of one's unique biography. The word *adulterated* is appropriate here, because it is the adult who interferes with the child's pure expression. Many grown-ups become unsettled when sitting still, prone to ignore the need for quiet time and introspection. It is in this fear that they hope to protect children from the same fate. Little do such parents realize that the solution lies with the child's rich inner life, an emotional state learned through the gift of independence and respected boundaries for both parties concerned. It must be recognized we need to protect children (**The Ones**) from undue adult interference. Their right to privacy is unassailable. Only in such an atmosphere can the truth of a vertical reality break through from higher spheres. What exemplifies these truths?

This brings me to a story of a little girl who was overjoyed with her baby sister just delivered. She requested of her parents that she be left alone with the newborn. Questioned why, she answered "Before she forgets, she will tell me the stories she brought down from heaven." I am reminded here that children are young human beings. Their soul processes of thinking, feeling, and acting are not developed to full maturity. This often evokes the impatience of a parent; however, no parent can assume that to be grown up makes one better. Children understand each other, and the bond between them is stronger then we as adults can ever imagine.

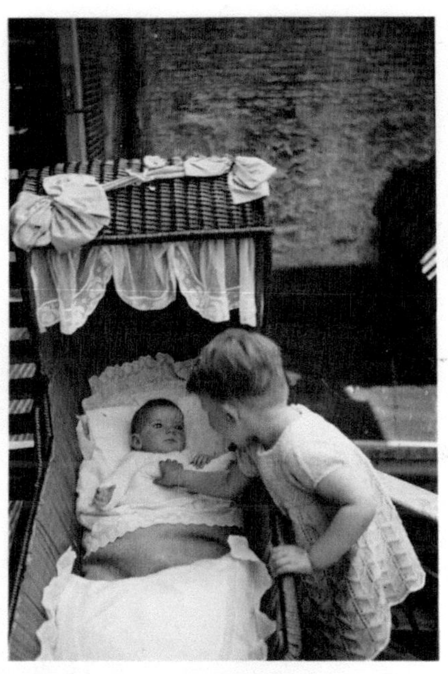

Plate 75: Two sisters

At the age of five, as a little girl, I was graced with a suprasensory clairaudient meeting. Far from this changing my life, I had the consciousness not only to experience the voice making a clear statement—"I WAS — I AM — I WILL FOREVER BE"—but also to question the voice as follows. *Anneke* (my childhood Dutch name), *do not forget this encounter. Here I stand. I am now five years old.* And while looking down on my little frame: *What am I going to do in this small female body?* An overwhelming burden is such a meeting where something larger makes one recognize the insignificance of the horizontal existence. Then the incident passes into the deep recesses of the child's soul, but it is never forgotten. It remained a biographical building block on which my whole life's philosophy could rest and later unfold. When I asked my father at the age of eight whether it is likely that we visit the Earth more then once, he immediately referred me to Indian religious texts in which spirit is accepted as an eternal entity and reincarnation is acceptable.

The choice of parent was "right on," is it not so? I as **The One** was protected but remained free from all indoctrinations during my growing years. Eventually, at the age of twenty-one, I had sufficient curiosity to study Theosophy, but I was not a joiner. So what really happened during this timeless experience? It was as if a part of me that I designated as a higher, wiser being wanted to remind me of the insignificance of mortality. Later I learned through the temple mysteries known in Spiritual Science about the meeting required from pupils during their initiation into Egyptian temples. The teacher, named here the Temple Hierophant, would guide the pupil in a near-death deep sleep, experienced for three days. Once moving in the astral world of the dead, the pupil meets The Sphinx, a crouching composite animal with a human head, a lion-like body, with the limbs and hoofs of a bull, its body having wings. Meeting the sphinx is an occult experience described as a path of initiation in the Egyptian temples more than three thousand years in the past. Again, it was the Hierophant as teacher and leader of the spiritual school who guided pupils in their final quest toward the spiritual initiation that afforded them deeper knowing of the "Self." The pupils would subject themselves to a temple sleep lasting three days. Extensive

Plate 76: Sphinx

training in physical hygiene, emotional restraint, and the understanding of the nether worlds (death) were all prerequisites that ultimately led to this final journey, a journey dedicated to the departed souls and an introduction to immortality. This being remained heavily veiled but revealed itself to students with a stern voice and the same declaration I was able to hear: *"I was—I am—I will forever be. No one shall lift my veil!"*

That last phrase, however, was a warning. What could the veil of secrecy be? Remember that these stringent rituals were performed thousands of years ago. The outcome was not always positive, for some postulants did not return from their visit to the nether world. Their sojourn during the temple sleep (astral world) could not be completed and they had to leave this world to reincarnate at a later date. That was exactly the secret of the veil! In those times any investigation into previous incarnations was strictly forbidden. So there is an evolutionary change in the spirit awakening.

The Magic Flute, the opera by Amadeus Mozart, gives an accurate reenactment of that journey. It was the sphinx who carried the secret of past and future lives behind the veil, the veil of forgetfulness. Can we lift that veil today through our own volition and inner work? How much has changed for the human beings born today in the West. Kali Yuga, the age of darkness, ended in the late eighteen hundreds. The veil of secrecy was lifted. Gone are the days of backroom séances, secret teachings from the East, and even spiritual consultants who pretend to know another person's previous lives. Independence in one's own spiritual journey is vouchsafed.

Immortality is a fact! This idea can be difficult for people to accept. An atheist living in the materialistic world has physical limitations, including the reality of death combined with the belief that no afterlife exists. It becomes the knowing that will give us certainty of life after death. Believing (religion) will not satisfy an inquisitive mind; belief does not offer certainty. To believe is a personally subjective sentiment that has no place in the study, exploration, and investigation of human potential and Truth. Do the knowers have to convince the believers or vice versa? That is a burning question for me and for perhaps all of those who were able to enter the higher worlds and gain glimpses of truths that could give meaning to earthly existence (ref. plate 29, page 32).

Do I have to convince another person about a reality of which they are unaware? Do I wait until they invite me into their own intimate inner explorations? When will a reversal in spiritual attitude manifest in the Western world? Are the natural sciences taught in our academic establishments the greatest distractors for young generations? The young also have to deal with the virtual realities offered by computers and the Internet. Will there eventually be a curriculum for young students that introduces them to Spiritual Science? This will happen only when students ask for it. I remain open-minded to all changes that the future might bring.

Experience with our Child Artist has given much support and an example for the future. His individuality is present in all his illustrations. He tells us of pre-earthly travels from far expanses, relationships with planetary hosts, and about his friend the "guardian angel." He has given evidence of lives in the past, during which he experienced research as an alchemist and gained remarkable knowledge of human genesis. No other person could present us with what he gave at this stage of his life. That personality still needed to unfold, requiring a span of another two times seven years. Only at the end of his twentieth year would that individual feel the urge to incarnate in the prepared vessel.

Seven-year Phases in Child Maturation

There is a logical interpretation of the biographical years used by spiritual scientists. When used, it brings order by labeling the periods of human development. It is known that the bodily cells have a seven-year renewal cycle. (Blood cells live much more briefly and take no part in this discussion.) If we can take this seven-year period as a ground rule, we could also imagine that we have received a new body at the age of seven (change of teeth), at fourteen (puberty and development of the sexual organs), and at twenty-one (social maturity). Being aware of the cosmic imprint on all of humanity, the planetary spheres of Moon, Mercury, Venus, Sun, Mars, Jupiter, and Saturn are reflected in this analysis. Understand that the physical bodies of these planets play no role, but the guidance and cosmic influences from those spheres are taken seriously.

With a living imagination, the Moon is identified as a reflector. Not only does it reflect information from Earth but also becomes the reflecting power for the whole universe. The metal connected with this body is silver. The brain is the organ of reflection in the physical body. As this function predominates in the first seven years we can deduce that it brings knowledge from cosmic spaces into the glue substance during the first seven years of child development. In sleep, the child's attention is focused on the Moon. Every moment the child loses itself in this sphere it receives instruction on how to build the physical body, strengthening memories and renewing connections with cosmic hosts. This intimate relationship ends with the falling out of the baby teeth. The Moon period functions as body builder.

Plate 77: Journey of "I" in sleep (0–21 years)

It is through the Tooth Fairy that a child is introduced to a higher sphere, that of Mercury. Development during the next seven years stands very much in the sign of Mercury, not the physical planet but a world of mercurial forces overseeing humanity from a higher dimension (cosmic spaces). These beings, as a part of the cosmic hierarchies, are recognizable in their gifts of good health, playfulness, and laughter, inducing a mercurial disposition in the child often bordering on banality, a sanguine nature sometimes inducing stealing that must not be interpreted as a moral defect in a child, but as an imitation of the god Mercury, the deity blessing traders, money-lenders, and thieves. Of course, mercury as a metal influences the life function in the physical body. We could introduce here the etheric body as the recognizable sheath beyond the physical, which is in need of attention in the developing human being.

Plate 78: God Mercury with winged feet

The lung is the organ imitating the properties of Mercury. Damage to the lung during these years can alter development, resulting in a lifelong pathology. In another chapter, we illustrated the mesmerizing, dynamic quality of this liquid metal. In its nature it resembles the dynamics of dispersion and consolidation—breath in, breath out. During the mercury period, ages of seven to fourteen, the life body, or etheric body, is structured to become an integral part of the constitution of **The One**.

Once the secondary sexual characteristics, feminine or masculine, begin to manifest, the developing teenager (**The One**) is ready for a promotion, so to speak, to a higher sphere (during sleep). Now the goddess Venus will appear in dream content and play an important role in the soul structure of the youth. She is the seducer, introducing lasciviousness; she rules over love and its compulsive sickness. She is the instigator of inappropriate behavior and socially unacceptable pranks. Her target organ is the kidney and the metal that personifies her being is the warm, lustrous, and highly conductive metal copper.

Sensing the maturing of the human being in her care, she induces (stimulates) the dialogue between opposites and asks for reason and wisdom to make independent choices. During these seven years, the astral body, the body of motion and emotion, is strengthened to incarnate, fashioning the independent personality. Increasingly, the personal identity shimmers through in the social activity, judgments, and predilections. Although seduction is a threat, overcoming these adversities strengthens the fiber of the personality.

Once the youth has traveled through these three spheres while sleeping, the twenty-one-year milestone has been reached. It follows from the foregone progression that the time has arrived for instruction of "I"—its strength, value, and goals are to be pursued. Only in the Sun sphere, with the lofty hosts of compassion, can such an education take place. At this point, further discussion of these stages is not needed for further illumination of this chapter.

Pictures from my own biography and case histories learned from practicing in a community for more than four decades can reflect truths and impress on the imagination. I am convinced that, as a relative outsider, sharing my experiences with the community that has become such an integral part of my life will bring, if rightly understood, joy in recognizing some truths and meaning. Most of all it could encourage all of us to heed the inner voice, reject skeptical naysayers, and become steadfast in recognizing the dormant inner strength in both young and old. That is spirit! My spirit adds value and meaning to an inner reality. As a continuous stream my life flows away, and only memories remain.

Frankly, at no time have I ever had an experience or distinct memory of past lives, but reason and inner knowing give me the certainty that no other possibility exists. This subjective experience is part of my Credo, intimately connected to the acceptance of the Christ in my life. In my imagination He is like an Alien, the Earth preparing a human body for him to dwell in for three years. During that time, he teaches the esoteric higher life that only a handful of disciples fathom. It will certainly take more than one life to comprehend the far-reaching consequences of His incarnation. Through my actions, my will, I desire to serve Him throughout time immemorial.

The question arises: How can I serve patients who request a consultation? It will suffice to act out of my personality, affability, and knowledge to diagnose, guide, and prescribe for them. As an individual, I see the individuality of patients and must meet them in a frame of destiny that brings constructive interaction. Patients come of their own volition or might be sent by unseen forces to work through a crisis. I often inquire about a patient's impulse to visit my medical practice. The frequent answer, astounding but not surprising, is that a clue was given to them in a dream. A picture emerges in which patient, doctor, and the spiritual world act out a relationship existing over a longer period of time through past incarnations, but also in consideration of the future.

Story of the Unbeliever

I feel impelled at this point to introduce a story illustrating a near-death experience (NDE) in a brilliant individuality with a strong denial of immortality or multiple earthly incarnations. Owing to a superior power of reasoning as a researcher interested in the social and economic sciences, he often requested extensive sessions during which we shared views on the eminent thinker, spiritual investigator, philosopher, and my teacher, Rudolf Steiner. The patient was a short, stocky man in his mid-sixties, evidently healthy, with enormous energy and focused decisiveness. He reminded me of a leader, familiar with giving orders and living a no-nonsense, orderly life. Meeting this individuality left a lifelong impression on me, and I valued his friendship enormously. He was an individual who appreciated the world of the sense-perceptible and who demanded discipline from those with whom he worked, because he himself was a disciplined, objective thinker.

As a connoisseur of life, the arts as represented in literature, music, and theater had his full attention. Throughout the years of the frequent encounters, I observed reticence in his revealing any subjective feelings concerning immortality. Like most hard-core scientists schooled in the best institutions of America, he denied the existence of experiences involving suprasensory occurrences. For him, the bodily nature was unassailable—once dead, existence ceases. Discussions on a dual nature—personal experiences not in the "flesh"—were easily discarded as subjective, not reproducible, insignificant, and a useless contribution to the human sciences. Topics I was interested in discussing included such questions as: What is life? How can it leave? Where does it go? Exact science requires answers, and we faced many dilemmas wherein sensory observation and scientific investigation could not reveal the answers to us.

He did heed the existence of an inner world, evidenced in his capacity to read to his wife every evening like clockwork. I cannot be sure whether the text was chosen by him or her. However, for a woman evaluating such activity from the outside, these are times that intimacies can blossom and be meaningful for a partnership. Such a gifted individuality must eventually encounter a meeting with another reality, more truthful and whole, opening the world of the spiritual kingdom beyond the familiar other three kingdoms. This meeting came to him as the specter of the being of cancer. Medical protocol advised surgical castration, to which he consented. As with the brilliant philosopher and theologian Peter Abelard, who lived in the eleventh and twelfth centuries, this humiliating surgery was performed and changed his life in unexpected ways. The path of transformation begins here, and we will explore this history to illustrate the capacity of a great, expansive soul.

My visit to the hospital was three days after his surgery. The recuperation was well within the expected parameters. During the previous night, however, there was an "incident" that prompted a follow-up visit the next day. Apparently he had taken a bath, to prepare for discharge, had fainted while rising out of the water, and hit his head against the rim, causing a deep laceration of the scalp. After being given a local anesthesia the wound was stitched, but his discharge was postponed for twenty-four hours. He was seventy-two years old. He shared with me an out-of-body experience, a separation from his body. He identified this as his consciousness, associated with his capacity to observe himself objectively from a corner in the room. He was standing in the bathtub, but his consciousness was not "in" it. He was riveted with surprise. A blissful feeling descended into or around him, knowing that he had completed his life, that there were no regrets or loose ends, and that now he could continue the journey that he desired to undertake. "Looking" back he saw his body crumbling, bending over, and with a loud explosive sound hitting the metal rim with his skull. It was as if this traumatic shock pulled him back into his body, overwhelming him with gravity, disappointment, and lament.

At no time did I offer any opinions or insights during the next three weeks, the time it took him to adjust to a rebirth on Earth as a different person. This was his journey and I assisted him by listening and observing the slow process of life that was teaching him higher realities. We know that the biography of the human being is divided into seven-year stages. What would normally take seven years in a human life, he undertook in seven days.

During the first day, he was incontinent and unable to stand. He could grasp objects and was able to feed from a bottle. He became aphasic after sharing his experience with me, a significant fact that favored the diagnosis of the patient undergoing an inner journey in contrast to a cerebral damage from the injury. On the second day, continence returned, and he was able to stand. By the end of the day he shuffled. I was at his bedside to observe. He wanted to be read to but chose picture books. He liked flowers but not sounds or strong odors. He sought frequent eye contact but still did not speak. The third day he showed remarkable improvement. He wanted to sit in a chair and feed himself. His sentences were like short orders. When I came through the door he greeted me with a bright smile. His family must have valued my visits, or perhaps he ordered them out of the room. At no time was there interference in this process of healing.

The wounds healed; there was no physical discomfort requiring sedatives, and his sleep was undisturbed. From the fourth day on, very slowly but deliberately his independence returned. His vocabulary had grown by leaps and bounds, his sentence structure became more mature, and he started to voice opinions about local events related to him by the family. There was no interest in the enterprise he had been connected to throughout his life. On the sixth day, he had a desire to revisit the incident in the hospital. The realization that he himself had experienced a dual existence, a fact he worked on by himself in the hours of solitude, was not easy for him to digest. At no time did he seek guidance in the spiritual sciences. His spiritual independence was at this time also a matter of pride and hanging on to a manhood that was only a memory. In his soul, he was seeking and finding meaning and adjusting to the burden of life. What do I have to live for? Not for name, not for fame, not for gain. There rises in me the need to play, and how can I project this change without upsetting family or caretaker?

There was a curious but subtle change in the second week. His body was healed, so there was no need for me to continue my visits, but at his insistence we continued the existing friendship and played chess and cribbage, his two favorite pastimes. He always won, and this irritated me to the hilt. I hate losing! But nothing was so astounding as when he opened Pandora's Box. Slowly, he revealed to me in greater detail the expansive experience in the short time of what I would call a loosening of the sheaths. We referred to this as The Bathroom Scene. The tableaux of his total life experience appeared as a panorama before and around him. At the time, it was a spontaneous phenomenon that awakened knowing in him that a continuation of life was certain. Steadfast in his Self, he sensed a completion of the life on Earth, realized the duality of his inner core, and accepted immortality as the absence of death. As he described it in humorous terms, "To die is to discard the physical body, the body that has served me so well during all these years." Being the eternally inquisitive scientist he wanted to explore what that box was all about! His experience was so vivid that the hours of focused contemplation following The Bathroom Scene made him realize that invisible realms will open up for the self if the idea of a dual existence can be toyed with. He was literally occupied by standing and walking in a world of thought. These invisible realms were made alive again through the imagination and memory of that incident, filling him with emotions far beyond daily experiences. What became internally alive was like a Greek myth, and I could play the role of the muse. The whole impression of his soul being, his strength, his rigidity, the rich characteristic structure of inheritance, was only a part of the being of two. That other part, the immortal aspect to which he was willing to concede, had no name yet. Was it Spirit?

His familiarity with theater, especially Shakespeare plays, which he could now study intensively, helped him identify previously unknown or rejected parts of himself. In the past, his higher Self, which I refer to as the "I," was working and organizing with a will to rule over the spirit instead of facilitating this spiritual entity to expand his world of knowing. The Spirit, when taken into consideration as an entity separate from the body, acquires independence of the body. He could immediately accept and "digest" this reality and the consequences that the aversion to spirit had on the evolutionary path of humanity. This diversion toward a one-sided development of powers of understanding provided by natural science awoke in him an urge to open within himself new paths of investigation. Did he have enough time?

After three weeks, we took our leave from each other. His knowing throughout the day consciousness—that a duality, a spirit being and his bodily being presented itself to the world—helped him to think and accept his own immortality. The cessation of function of one part does not mean the demise of the spiritual part. The reality that eventually he would be freed from motion and emotion opened up exciting and interesting possibilities. His last words to me were, "Let us be open to learn what comes after my [death], a world where I will meet you again!"

For three years all interaction between us ceased, but he was good to his word. One evening he phoned to inform me of the progression of his disease. He made an inquiry as to a certain medicine he had saved over the three years of his retirement. Much thinking was exchanged. Little was said. Early the next morning my eternal friend and patient came to me to say Fare well! His presence was palpable as a spatial force field.

There is no question about the nature of the dying process as part of The Bathroom Scene that my patient had to undergo. *Excarnation* is another term frequently used in Spiritual Science for the near-death experience.

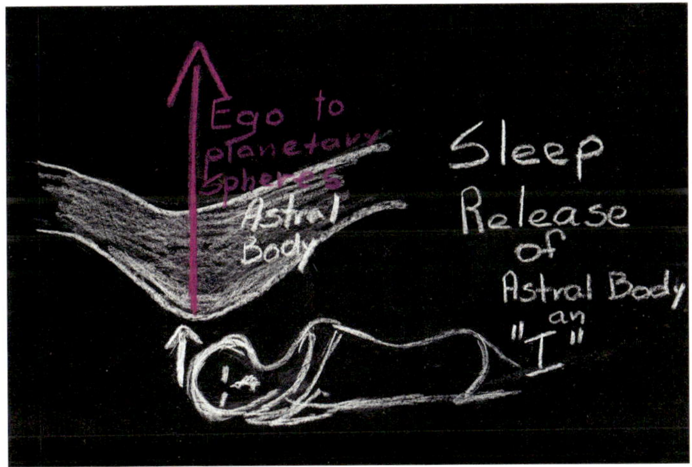

Plate 79: Sleep and separation of astral body and "I"

As previously explained, I refer to the four sheaths, or veils, as phenomena that compose of the human constitution. Under certain conditions such as fainting, near-drowning, or poison ingestion, the sheaths around an organ or the whole body loosens. The first sheath to separate is the denser, watery entity, also called the etheric (or life) body. In the case of total separation, the physical body is deprived of the protection of its life-bestowing function and will proceed to the death process. Deprivation of oxygen sets in motion a cascade of deathly biochemical reactions. One wonders if the combining of the atom C with the atoms N and H to form the deathly HCN (hydrogen cyanide) molecule in the absence of oxygen could play a role.

The phenomena of experiences that occur in connection with the separation of the etheric body are described in many NDE. How many people talk about that beautiful tableau, a sum total of the memories accumulated throughout their whole life? This appears around the person in a colorful display, things long forgotten, states of vulnerability, sadness, joy, and harm perpetrated to others, now remembered through this body of memory and mercifully left behind when the individuality (**The One**) travels up and on. Most people who have experienced this phenomenon do not understand the miracle and are quickly able to forget it.

The reason for my patient showing a reticence in discussing it was his need to weigh the experience in his own mind. For days he was occupied with reviewing, giving careful examination, and obviously failing to find points of reference without considering the existence of Spirit. This was indeed no laughing matter, yet in the second week he received help from his own new constitution, mercurial as it was then, and inevitably his own fully present individuality as an eternal infinite flame was embraced.

The discussion and experience of the etheric body separating from physical body brings me to question whether a similar life-changing scenario can unfold with the astral body. An awakened state, being aware of my surrounding with a continuous feedback from the senses can give me the impression that an unconscious life does not exist. Yet most of us are bombarded daily by negative emotions, feelings of stress, frustration, anger, anxiety, and loss of joy—in other words, the unknown world of passive experiences to which we have submitted. The world of the unconscious wells up through the veils of daily activity, and the astral body (as the body of emotion) experiences these hindrances. Thus the content of the astral body is not only what is remembered from past and present consciousness, but also the part hidden in the "unconscious." The explorations made into the hidden nature and the unrevealed aspects of the personality fall in the domain of psychology. The submerged life of habits, suppressed trauma of childhood, and dreams are all food for analysis during therapeutic counseling by a psychologist.

During sleep, the body of emotions and consciousness thereof has separated from the body. While in an induced coma, no memories or dreams are retraceable. In a state of sleep, however, dreams reveal valuable information of unconscious soul hurdles to us. Carl Jung (1890–1962), a Viennese physician and psychologist, did groundbreaking work on the psyche of the European soul and, through unceasing reconstruction of his own journey into his unconscious, identified the importance of the collective unconscious and "dream work." Through numerous publications and through his methods in counseling, Jung inspired many followers who were seeking to free themselves from such soul restraints. The treatment protocol demanded weekly visits over years. What could be attained during these sessions? Jungians (as his students and followers were called) were not acquainted with Spiritual Science and did not

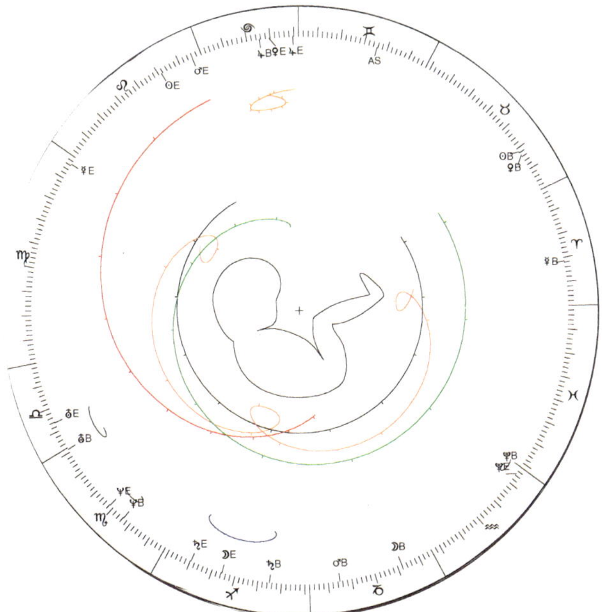

Plate 80: Zodiac belt around the fetus

acknowledge the concept of the astral body—naming this bodily sheath after the celestial spheres, which brings consciousness (emotions and willed movement), most likely derives from ancient sages. From antiquity, we bring knowledge of the Zodiacal belt to modern astrology, which includes the twelve segments occupying the heaven's circumference, most of which are connected with animal names. True to the recognition in Anthroposophy, even these far-distant cosmic spaces, positioned like a belt around our solar system, have imponderable influences on human beings. The old masters still knew and assigned the heavenly regions as being the home of creator gods, who also endowed us with the vices, hurdles in our soul-response that we will have to transform into virtues during our many lifetimes on Earth. Virtuous individuals—those who have overcome many vices through many lives on Earth—can be recognized by others who walk their path on Earth as human beings who are upright, honest, loyal, without greed and jealousy, and, foremost, cultivate love for fellow human beings and aim toward freedom.

Throughout the ages, religious institutions have prodded humanity's conversion by advocating a life that imitates the "Savior." Now, humanity has entered a stage of evolution in which the process of purifying the vices of the astral body will be an individual conscious activity within the soul. Repetitive evening evaluations of one's own stumbles during the daily experiences of life contributes to the cleansing process. Such a task was a part of temple and cloistered life. A process of personal awakening and desire for development and maturation replaces outer pressures. Much from the past will be rejected, but the truth and knowledge of our human relationship with the heavens grows stronger.

The human being as **The One** is a space-occupying body at the moment of birth, when a child takes the first breath. The positions of constellations are exact in time and space, meaning that each human being is imprinted with a unique celestial pattern in the astral body, the body equipped to receive and hold onto this cosmic reality. I marvel to think that the guidance and direction given to us from cosmic spaces is so organized that the desired virtue to be attained in an incarnation is connected with a zodiacal region.* To decide the timing of birth under the guidance of cosmic forces means to choose a vice given to us through the zodiacal imprint.** Of course this is also the springboard for all the popularized astrological manipulations directed by earthbound, materialistic thinking.

In the beginning, after my conversion to the practice of medicine extended by Anthroposophy, understanding the astral body was an urgent need. This body, through which emotions and movements manifest, is elusive mainly because conventional training blinds us with a belief that the personality designates our character, spiritual matters, and relationships to our ancestors, family, and friends. The study of psychiatry and psychology could not reveal the true secret behind mental disorders. Natural science faces closed doors when the human psyche is researched, the results of which are expressed in terms of brain enzymes, genetic disposition, and the latest cutting-edge theories.

A clear distinction between the personality and the individuality is not grasped. The personality is largely the product of family, genetic disposition, religious orientation, and geographic location. For the child, these factors become the support system and imprint a future adult emotional and soul life. In a previous chapter you were encouraged to form an image of the human being experiencing a two-dimensional plane. For people in general, the horizontal plane refers to their role in the family, work and vocation, and social position. Getting stuck in this dimension, trusting only conscious experience, satisfying impulses, and receiving affection from the surrounding world will not complete the factor of happiness. Facilitating the inherent soul power of thinking, feeling, and willing, the interaction between the world around me and my own being will assume a whole new dimension of give and take. Most human beings think primarily

---

* See, for example, Steiner, *Man and the World of the Stars: The Spiritual Communion of Mankind;* also, Hilton, *Speaking to the Stars: An Introduction to Astrosophy.*

** Steiner, *The Challenge of the Times,* lect. 3, p. 103.

of themselves first. Being human with many transactions to handle during the day, I hear these words; "What is in it for me?" Becoming conscious of this interference is the first step of self-growth. Reviewing these thoughts at the end of the day is a mandate for developing an intense feeling life in which, increasingly, the stumbles we make become conscious reminders for correction. Only with compassion instead of guilt can I as a person learn to accept my personal shortcomings. With the will to embrace the rhythm of the daily review, the next day will bring a change in what we encounter. We can transform those short repetitive inner jolts such as, "Who does she thinks she is?" "I feel put down!" "I will annihilate you!" "Why her and not me?" "Nothing goes right for me." "Poor Me!"

On the horizontal plane, our tools are thinking, feeling, and a will to act. Behavioral therapy can bring changes and relief to my patient, but without the introduction of the existence and ultimate recognition of the unique individuality the patient remains "unwhole" and in a state of limbo.

Simply put, I have a body; I am not my body. This is followed by, I have a soul when thinking, feeling, and acting, but I am more than a soul function. It is staggering for me to realize how many patients seek help and become truly ill because of physical as well as soul imbalances. By this I mean imbalance among one's thinking, feeling, and willing and a lack of control over the latter functions. Only through a path of Spiritual Science can I be introduced to the fact that an individuality exists behind the personality. This explains my preoccupation with these two planes—the horizontal and the vertical. The horizontal earthly dimension—existence in time and space and bound by earthly limitations—was described in the previous paragraphs. I can use my focused attention when describing the expansion into a vertical stream and identify with the concept of inner knowing. In a state of quietness when thinking is stilled or focused, an outside power flows in and meets the core of my being. I recognize existence beyond daily life. The tools of my perceiving are the transformation from my focused thinking into imagination, from feelings into inspiration, and from my will into the capacity for intuition.

Silence is the condition for opening to the vertical dimension. This conversation or exchange with entities in this vertical existence, gives me the capacity to embrace Spiritual truths and the facility to unite with higher beings. The subtle embrace with the gods clarifies the saying: "It thinks in me." Suddenly I can let go of the lower self's desire to be first, most important, and the center of attention.

Recognition that my individuality has no gender in higher spheres merging with a Totality beyond naming, and awakening to my own duality and assignment in the earthly sphere makes me an eternal citizen in the creation. My higher self has an unending love, tolerance, and enthusiasm for the activity and goals I am attempting to fulfill while living my life as a human being. As a guide the world of Spirit leaves me the guardian angel, the being that protects me in my vulnerability, both physical and psychological, throughout my life. Do you have the feeling that you are watched from above? Do you have a certainty of someone keeping you out of trouble? Only in the growth of the personality while on Earth can **The One** evolve from the state of interdependence with the Godhead and develop the urgent volition to take over the evolution and responsibility for all of humanity. Jesus was caught up in a dispute when he said that those who follow an "esoteric path" will be gods (John 10:34). I know this promise is pending. Whatever was meant, of course, is open to our imagination

Let us revisit the Emerald Tablet. It mentions the movement of **The One** between Earth and Heaven. It is described in postulate seven. *It ascends from Earth to Heaven, and then returns back to Earth. So that it receives the power of the upper and the lower.* The combined excarnation of the astral body and the "I" is attained in deep meditation, while asleep, during a fainting spell, in an induced coma as with anesthesia, or following a brain injury. A state of "sleep" guarantees the visit of the "I" and astral body to the heavens.

It is comforting to know that in all these cases there is a literal ascent to the heavenly home, an astral plane, a dimension filled with beings and regions that will protect the kernel of the vulnerable body-free existence. That is my plea for protection whenever I leave my physical and life body behind and in the care of a circumstance I am unable to control. This pendulum swinging between Heaven and Earth is possible by dint of the body layers, their independence while existing in other dimensions, creating opposite realities humanity will eventual recognize as follows:

1) A state of forgetfulness and a state of wakefulness when memories accumulate
2) Living in two worlds—one as the earthly dweller, one as the initiate of astral planes where other dimensions are introduced

The earthly home is bound to time and space and requires perception and soul expression. In the heavenly home, where sense activity is left behind, our instruments of experience are imagination, inspiration, and intuition. Here the declaration of the Wise One, Hermes Trismegistus, that power is received in both worlds becomes clear. While on Earth in a wakeful state, I can develop power out of my own volition—power to will, power to control my destructive thoughts and feelings, power to do good, power to sacrifice. Once I am asleep, however, I will receive the knowing from a spiritual sphere, delivered to me, not out of nothingness, but in a dimension with the presence of departed souls and heavenly hosts. How many of us have received messages from departed loved ones through dreams? I can declare the power that will eventually belong to all of humanity, the power of the oneness in all. This illumination can be worked for while in the earthly dimension. Many of us know it, search for guidance, and explore possibilities, even through drug-induced states. I have explored these examples on other pages.

Story of the Believer

The work in self-discovery has to be undertaken on the path of healing or acquiring a balance in daily life. Patients with a terminal disease such as cancer can decide to choose an alternative treatment that includes intense self-exploration whereby the "I" wills itself to find the origin of the imbalance through dream analysis. Such a patient visited Pleroma Farm, a therapeutic farm in Hudson, New York, that blossomed for seven years as a retreat for persons in search of a spiritual path in their recovery of health. My patient's process of healing becomes an illustration of how Spiritual Science can open a pathway to feel the power of "mind over matter." Her story follows.

It is remarkable to realize the hundreds of hours that Carl Jung, as a psychiatrist and researcher, dedicated to the unconscious, unraveling the hidden emotional life with the help of collective stories and human dreams, addressing the imbalanced soul, or what I designate as the astral world. My patient, from whom I could learn so much, was a Jungian analyst. She was born in Canada to a father who was a blue-collar worker and a mother who lived vicariously through this younger daughter. Our patient, fifty-six years old, was sensitive, cultured, artistic, and endowed with extraordinary beauty and purity. The mother had dedicated herself to the dance career of this second daughter beginning at the age of five and did not let up until she became a ballerina. She was coerced at a young age and in bondage to the compulsive dreams of a parent. She did indeed become professional and later opened a ballet school, but could not find a trustworthy comfortable partner until her late forties. She'd had no pregnancies.

At the age of forty-nine, she was diagnosed with uterine cancer, which was a wake-up call. She decided to search for healing without the conventional interventions. Consequently, major changes in her biography were registered. She left the dancing profession, followed a three-year course in Jungian analysis, accepted a guide for her own soul exploration, and began an intensive discipline in dream analysis. After seven years, although her physical health was not a concern to her, a physical examination revealed a walnut-size pelvic tumor for which all modern treatment was rejected. Instead she came to Pleroma Farm to acquaint herself with the medical practice and therapies extended by Anthroposophy. After a treatment protocol was established, the use of the remedies, injections, therapeutic eurythmy, and counseling was administered. She established a visit twice a year for seven years.

The most important work done during the first visit, which was a forty-day retreat, involved careful intensive study of the biography.* Each seven-year block from birth was examined, each in a different light according to the journey her astral body undertakes during sleep. The experience for the patient meant plunging into a world of unknowns in which the "I" objectively unravels the dynamic interaction between her and the family she chose as a vehicle of incarnation. She learned that the dreams guiding her each night may reflect the intense work of memory retrieval in that stage of her life. The patient and the guide start to explore feelings toward the parents. Her father was a gentle submissive man whom she adored. (*The dream here was a fishing scenario. Both persons are standing on the bank of the river. He hooks a big fish and prepares a meal for her.*) Her mother, the dominant caregiver, gave her the dream of dance and could make that reality come true through enormous sacrifice of her own life task. Exploring mother-daughter relationships, whereby a vicarious transference of mother over daughter is witnessed, awakens the reality that the existing pathology is intertwined with the combined feminine axis—the mammary glands and pelvic gonads. For her, it was impossible to create a distinct, strong energy around her own feminine axis, and she finally succumbed to a malignant invasion in the pelvis. Shortly after her mother passed at the age of ninety-four, the patient's transition followed.

* See O'Neill, *Human Destiny.*

The goal in therapy for patients with an incurable disease is to expand the power of their being. The big fish that the father prepared as a meal—that is power! When I have to face the transition, "What will give me strength and power to go over the threshold?" What gives strength is when the patient can answer these questions: "Who Am I?" "What is my past, present, and future?" I gain power from knowing the effect each unique being has on me. "How will people remember me?" "What is the legend I leave behind?" "What is my unique essence that I can take as a gift for the hosts in heaven?"

For seven years the conversations during treatments continued. Physically the tumor progressed to become a stage class IV. When her mother finally died at the age of ninety-four, permission to finalize her earthly existence was explored and finally

Plate 81: Birthday

activated. Her last gift to me was an exquisite small piece of artwork titled *The Birthday*.

Reexamining my experiences with her through the years, a question arose: What can I remember her by? It is this artistic jewel! I scrutinize, coming to the realization only now: she knew all along her own destiny, cosmic journey and infinite existence. The certainty of accomplishment true to the beauty she was able to represent while on Earth in dance, in painting, and in the social succor shared with so many human beings. Fully aware of spirit, she understood the Spiritual Sciences and traveled unencumbered in the dimensions that lay ahead of her. Here the believer becomes the knower.

The spiritual path of such an individual must include the certainty of immortality. Being a physician and understanding the medical profession very well, especially how loath we are to bring the truth of imminent "death" to the patient or the family, we make room for the help of a religious counterpart. But few of us have an understanding of Spiritual Science and the certainty this knowledge can bring to the patient. Ultimately that becomes the goal, knowing that rest, peace, and final expiration will come to all. When that time comes, how will we embrace it? My deepest nature, as with every human being, comes from above, not from the Earth. I use consciousness to direct a healing process. What are signs of healing? Is euthanasia—an act or resolve made through the patient's free will—an indication of healing? It still takes enormous courage and a strong will to go blindly where only uncertainties face you. Or are there no uncertainties for such individuals? These are only bare hints as to what spiritual guiding is about. When a patient and I are together, I strive for recognition of the imponderable element to assist in the struggle of seeking balance. Failure is not the return of the cancer in my patient; failure would be, for example, my rejection of the patient's decision to terminate her or his life. Yet freedom of will and strengthening the power of **The One** is the ultimate goal of these writings.

Euthanasia will become an obstacle for the future. Today in Western medicine, especially through the practice of hospice care, patients are assisted in dying with the help of pain medication. Suicide could be judged as an ethical issue. The family and environmental repercussions are graver then we think. Assisted suicide is legal in some U.S. states, in Canada, and in some European countries. This becomes an ethical issue. The conscious will of the patient is my professional consideration. As long as I withhold my consent, I cannot assist them in the process of transition. We might all agree that **The One**, present in another dimension beyond, awaits the merger with its lower "I." The guardian protects us in our transition. Immortality is the core theme of this section in which infinite existence and reincarnation are considered. The question needs to be stated: *Is* ***The One*** *in control of its own birth and death?*

When I was young and had no consciousness of Spirit birth occurring at the same time as conception, I was in agreement with abortion. Knowing the miracle of **The One** through the study of embryo genesis, the existence of the human being before birth, and the eagerness for it to experience incarnation into a material world weighs heavy on my shoulders. Pro-life should not only be a political football but an informed consent to take responsibility for **The One** and make incarnation possible. Subjectively it becomes a personal choice of the pregnant woman, a responsibility toward herself and the child's destiny. Objectively it is a matter of Law.

We end this chapter with a picture given to me by one of my patients, donated to my collection of *suprasensory occurrences*. Forty days after grannie's passing, this photograph of the grave was taken.

Plate 83: Granny's grave

Prometheus

Like thee, Man is in part divine,
A troubled stream from a pure source;
And Man in portions can foresee
His own funereal destiny;
His wretchedness, and his resistance,
And his sad unallied existence:
To which his Spirit may oppose
Itself—and equal to all woes,
And a firm will, and a deep sense,
Which even in torture can descry
Its own concenter'd recompense,
Triumphant where it dares defy,
And making Death a Victory.

—Lord Byron

Sound O

In this section, experience of the O formation in gesture and sound are examined as a testimony to the footstep of **The One** on Earth. In the sound O, **The One** learns to experience an inward gesture of containment and boundaries, self-reliance, trust in the community, and hope for the future. In the English language, many words containing the O sound project the energy of comfort and inclusion but also an objective reality of aloneness. The language speaks and has a formative activity on life processes that can be demonstrated through the transformative powers of eurythmy.

Throughout the writings in this book, pivotal attention is given to **The One**. The Child Artist at the age of six reminds us of what our journey of earthly incarnation involves. The beginnings of existence are found in the infinite past, but it is in the present that an invitation is extended for all of us to explore the essence of **The One**.

Human beings each have to consider one's authentic name as the "I," the first step toward freedom. No one has permission to cross the boundary of the O, with which **The One** surrounds and protects itself. Through the choices made by **The One**, sharing becomes a conscious act that reveals the most intimate confessions—those of past indiscretions or personal failures, but also confessions of faith and reconciliation as exemplary "food" for changing habitual behavior and collectively destructive patterns.

In today's culture and the development of the consciousness soul,* reintroduction to Hermes Trismegistus, a master of the past, and his Emerald Tablet postulate "*As above so below...*," can reconnect humanity to a truth needed for future choices, behind which **The One** can stand. We learn anew that the confluent flow from above toward **The One** is a reality.

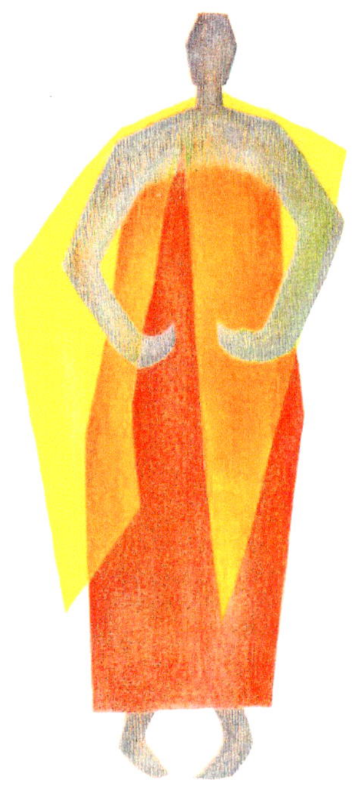

Plate 84: Eurythmy gesture of O

The personal path through the seven-year periods, the roles of woman, mother, doctor, and lover are all intimate O experiences that become a part of one's biography and a testimony to authenticity. This section offers examples of how human beings can attend to themselves in a earthly biographies as **The One**—as members of humanity. Objective recognition of **The One** is in seeing the "other." Subjective recognition of **The One** is identifying one's own individuality.

The physical body must become an obedient instrument for **The One**, working in and through it. The constitution of the human body is subject to a continuous structural change during the cycles of days, months, and the years, and, as we know, in each seven-year cycle a completely renewed cell structure manifests. Purification, refinement, and detoxification of physical substances are organic processes assigned to alchemical science, a school of knowledge now replaced by the science of biochemistry. Understanding Alchemy (introduced in "Sound A") could develop an imagination whereby these processes are pictured as a

* Steiner, *An Outline of Esoteric Science*, p. 46f.

continuous activity in our interior, so that the concept of self-healing could be embraced as an integral part of bodily activity. An example would be, for instance, a body responding with high fever as a mechanism to burn out and rid itself of an invasion. The concept of self-healing is of great significance because of the power of trust that is given to **The One** who chooses to assert such freedom in its own life.

The One needs to conceive its soul as an organ. Evolutionary development is assigned in mounting steps from sentient, to intellectual, and to conscious soul capacities throughout thousands of years of world history. The soul activity of **The One** as a representative of humanity is limited to two conscious experiences.* The capacity to reason belongs only to the human soul. At an early age **The One** is guided to judge and choose between opposites—for instance, the *yes* or the *no*. Challenges and choices foster growth in the organ of the soul. A spontaneous capacity for love and hate is a purely human experience and becomes the second attribute of the human soul. Through the presence of the organ of soul, **The One** experiences desire and can react impulsively to stimuli arising from either conscious or unconscious influx. Embroidering with these two capacities, love/hate and reason, the soul as an independent emoting entity receives stimuli from two sources.

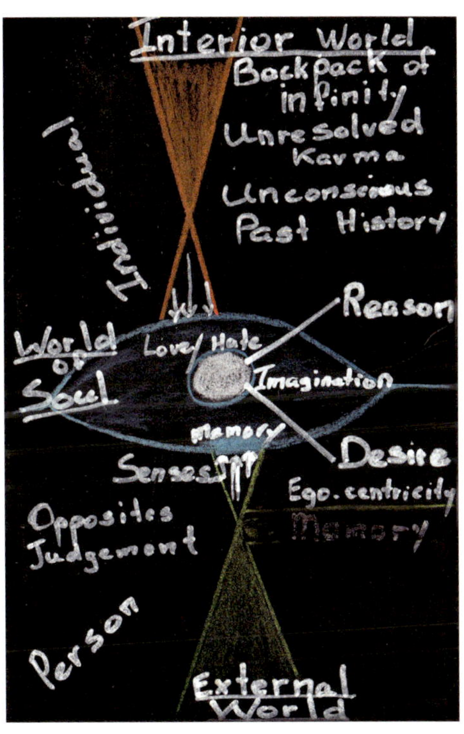

Plate 85: Soul as an organ

* Steiner, *A Psychology of Body, Soul, and Spirit,* p. 80.

First, one recognizes that perceptions through the sense organs provide a continual source of stimulation for the soul, "bombarding" the exterior border of the soul organ, even during sleep. The organs of the senses are not a part of the soul but affect the soul life continually. On one side, **The One** has to deal with sense impressions that contribute a great deal to the content of its soul force. An impulse of desire arises from an interior place deep within or beyond this organ and flows and mingles with the outer impressions to create a soul constitution that is unique to the personality of **The One**.

Desire arises from deep regions of soul to meet the reality of opposing stimuli—polarities in the world. Light or dark, warm or cold, wet or dry, silent or noisy are all conditions that stimulate the senses, creating perceptions that in turn inundate the boundary between the outside and interior worlds. Steeped in such controversy, the soul experience must represent a "*battlefield upon which struggles are in progress*" (Steiner). Guidance in childhood becomes a responsibility toward **The One**'s expression of a life of desire, frustrations, controversy, as well as feelings of love and wonder. These need to be recognized by adults in the child-being. The percepts created by the sense organs, whether sound, image or odor, are registered by the soul organ and create a memories. Memory formation is a secondary reaction to percepts flowing in from the outer world through one's boundaries to become part of the inner soul experience. Memory is not a soul function; it is created by the world of senses.

The force of reason—solely a human activity—becomes the second pure soul function next to the feelings of attraction or aversion. Although visual perception is not a function of the soul, the capacity for visualizing images conjured up by dint of reason remains a pure unadulterated soul element.

Only after full maturation after the age of twenty-one does **The One** identify with a life task. As personalities, which begin to manifest at sexual maturation, human beings have not yet mastered themselves but remain bound to their own reactions to the environment and social surroundings. After the age of three times seven, with the birth of the "I" at twenty-one, an interior force presents itself—a force that identifies one's "I" as a separate entity. This awakens **The One** to ideologies it wishes to pursue, enabling people to discover their life tasks. Here the exercise of writing a credo will be helpful (see page 158). Reasoning, using the power of deduction, exercising logic in the development of questions, and experiencing the light and triumph of humanity's higher purpose is an inherent quality of the soul, spurred on by higher realms. Here, the soul is used as instrument of action while incarnated on Earth. **The One**, as a representative of humanity, functions in its individuality.

The soul, as a derivative of the human being, represents one part of the trinity (spirit, soul, and body) and is, so to speak, juxtaposed between Heaven and Earth. On Earth, the life of desire finds its activity, expressed by the person in reaction to outer life. From higher regions, an eternal aspect of the human is represented in the capacity to identify one's individuality through reason and examination and perhaps through the practice of a religious discipline. Why?

Throughout life, people are out of balance in soul activity—that is, dissociation exists among the three expressions of thought, feeling, and will. Often, chaotic and disturbing thoughts overwhelm our daily tasks. Experiences of pain, sadness, or fear play into soul as discomfort attributable to that imbalance. The effort of will is too weak to dominate the incongruities of the companion soul functions, feeling and thinking, which in turn cause discomfort. This hinders the personality from fully expressing the authentic self on Earth—its purpose and its connection with humanity, as well as the desire to maintain and remember one's divine origin. Perhaps one can gain a connection through a religious discipline. This is only the barest hint of what wants to become spiritual. To unite with the divine is the most intense experience that the soul can attain. Have many Earth dwellers succeeded in reaching that state? There are testimonies of postulants in both East and West searching and occasionally approaching a "heaven," being "surrounded by sublime white light," finding "ecstasy," or resting in the Heart of God—in other words, consciousness in which all is encompassed in One. Experiencing Light and Bliss is objective. Naming God is purely subjective.

The Emerald Tablet reminds us of the inevitability that each of **The Ones** will ascend from the Earth to a higher reality. So we can pose these questions: What is the time period of such a journey? Are there schools "up there"? What will we learn? Why ever come back to Earth? To answer these questions means studying Spiritual Science. Research by inquisitive minds and finding answers have always been possible—whether in the Schools of Tibet or in ancient temples of Babylon, Egypt, and Greece. Most of humanity was forbidden to lift the veil of spiritual truths, because such knowledge had to remain hidden. With the end of Kali Yuga, the time of secrecy ended and humanity now stands on the threshold of mysteries freely revealed.

These truths are the essence of **The One**:

1) Immortality: after excarnation (death) a journey through the solar system begins. In each sphere, the relinquishment of memories occurs as they are left "behind."
2) Reincarnation: insight into multiple earthly lives and an introduction to past and future lives on Earth.
3) Creative progress for the human being toward ultimate perfection, executed by the hierarchies in the likeness of the Godhead.
4) Spiritual Evolution: human beings develop the capacity for love and freedom.
5) Metamorphosis: changes in the physical human body occur to accomplish these goals.

This stipulates a future journey in which training will be needed. The information regarding the expansion of our spiritual being in celestial spheres does not come from books or religious institutions or even, for that matter, from Earth. The knowing we need exists already within all of us.

The Child Artist knows and leads us and remembers our tutelage in the heavens. I cannot do other than listen and share this information with the reader. As we have noticed from the Child Artist's drawings, considerable knowledge is connected to embryonic development. Cells are directed in a dance, currents of dynamic activity of restraint or deployment, choosing functions and moving to positions in the small organism where optimum responses create form and function. The one who is doing the directing is the embryonic incarnating being, **The One**.

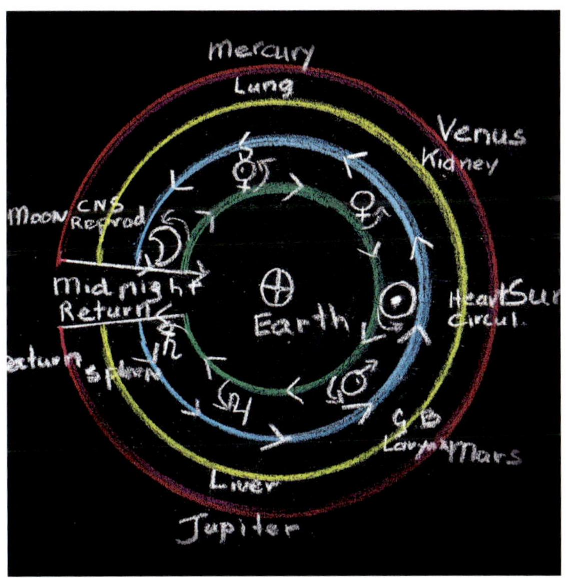

Plate 86: Leaving behind karma in each sphere

In death we part with the restrictive earthly body. Our journey through our universe can be undertaken as a path similar to the journey human beings experience while asleep. There are visitations, successively, to the spheres of Moon, Mercury, Venus, Sun, Mars, Jupiter, and Saturn until, in the end, we dwell in the bosom of Saturn. Imagine that the hierarchies on these celestial bodies are occupied only with expanding an individual's understanding. This understanding of functions and forms is connected with the physical body and the soul. We receive an exchange from each sphere according to the organs we fashion. For example, the Moon gives us knowledge of brain and reproductive organs. The next sphere of influence is represented by Mercury, a powerful impulse to the formation of the lung. Venus exerts influence on the kidney system formation and does interfere with the gender issue. Our circulatory system exists as a whole under the dominating influences of the Sun. Mars and its beings educate us on the use of our voice through the larynx and on the dominant role of the bile in digestion. The beings of the Jupiter sphere know the domination of the water, which is regulated by our largest organ, the liver. The Saturn sphere concludes the ring of planetary existences in our solar system, with its forces influencing the spleen in the rhythms of digestion and the physical body. The spleen system is little understood physiologically and might play a more significant role in a future transformed body.

The Experience in O for a Person on Earth

In the sound of O, the commonality of all humanity will be celebrated. Each of us as a personality has a place on this Earth. True, none of us are similar. We choose gender distinction and a genetic disposition, combined with a specific time of incarnating that meets the needs for expressing ourselves in a challenging world of opposites. Standing in a circle and holding hands, figuratively speaking, expresses a willingness to accept differences and even welcome those humans on Earth whose actions and habits can teach us tolerance and perseverance.

Even an agnostic has a credo. People need to identify with their particular background, understand the opportunities offered by the environment, and come to know their personal potential and limitations through education so that the world can be influenced and changed for the better. The credo becomes a confession of the faith one has combined with an undying dedication to this reality.

The contact we have with suprasensory worlds is still subjective and does not make one a superior person. What becomes outstanding in a biography is the person's recognition of vices and the steps that one can take to transform these negatives into something positive—namely, the virtue connected as the opposite of the vice. The strength of self-help groups (AA, for example) can be found in community gatherings around those in need and who declare and confess both helplessness and compassion. "There but for the Grace of God go I." Only with the utmost discretion of the participants can trust be built—trust deserved by all the persons living, working, and playing together. The energy of an O gesture becomes stronger with the acceptance of differences in each person. Each person is unique, thank God! The asset of each and every one lends beauty to the tapestry. A person can emulate but not imitate. There is a world of difference between those two concepts.

Gender

I want the reader first of all to understand that gender differences are real and explained in the following discussion, which illustrates anatomical and physiological as well as soul distinctions between male and female persons—knowledge that all need to acquire as **The One**. As for me, I questioned the impact my role as a female physician has had on my surroundings.

Plate 87: Cellular penetration by the life forces

It is remarkable that the gamete as the male and female reproductive cells is prepared long before fertilization with only half of the chromosomes so that, in the process of fusing, the expected forty-six chromosomes are present. The male gamete (spermocyte cell) carries fifty percent XY and fifty percent XX chromosomes. The sperm determines gender when a XX+XX merger develops a female body or XX+XY a male body.

All living human cells are penetrated or suffused by the etheric body, which has the capacity to utilize formative forces to affect life processes. Is there a distinction found in living formative forces between the male and female organization? Yes, which is partly why I want to explain the differences in greater depth. As we can deduce from foregoing texts, nature's activity finds its order in fourfold adherence to the elements of warmth ether, light ether, chemical ether, and life ether. These are called formative forces. Each of the four forces has distinct characteristics. In the warmth and light ethers, we find centrifugal, radiating qualities. These two ethers are actively productive, transmuting substances and life affirming. By contrast, the chemical and life ethers have centripetal tendencies of absorption and a tendency to embrace or enclose (an O gesture) within, reflecting indolence and the quality of water-retention.

The feminine with this distinct nature tends to be portrayed as passive and receptive. We can deduce that these two distinct opposite qualities will have a designation in the gender psychology of the human being. It is popular to say men are from Mars, women are from Venus. Let's see if this distinction has a leg to stand on.

In our understanding of the sleeping body, two distinct entities come into play. One is the solid corporal structure and the other the life-asserting and imponderable flow of forces in all living tissues (also referred to as living water). As with the differentiation in the sexes, the forces working with the corporal structure are diametrically opposite; the physical difference between male and female is undeniable. What the sexes are endowed with in their psychological activity is not so clear in these modern times. First, as in the case of the gamete, the formative forces are split, with warmth and light ethers functioning in one pole of the body, and the chemical and life ethers influencing the other pole—the head and genital poles in this case. The male genital pole adheres to the formative forces of the warmth and light ethers, where it exerts its true nature of activity, enthusiasm to burst out and impregnate the surroundings. The female genital pole attracts the opposite formative forces, those of chemical and life ethers, and becomes preoccupied with the passive and receptive formative forces.

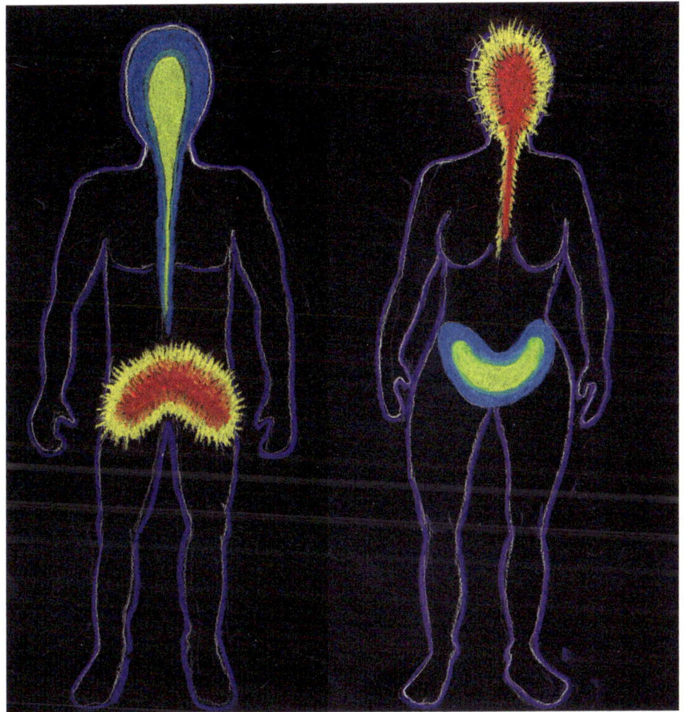

Plate 88: Polarities of the pelvis vs. head of male (left)
Plate 89: Polarities of the pelvis vs. head of female (right)

Laws of nature ensure that those formative forces of the etheric body not applied to the maintaining of the corporal structure are used to assert influence on the opposite pole, the head. *What is not used as formative force in the corporal function within the organism will serve as free forces yielding a psychological and spiritual influence on the person's thought processes.* The spiritual and psychological function arising from the free-flowing formative forces stimulate the head region of the two genders, each in a specific way. The head forces in the male differ from those in the female. Subjectively, as a female I have discovered throughout life that my thought processes are distinctly different from those of the opposite sex. The female can draw on the free-flowing formative forces that arise from the light and warmth ethers. Flamboyant imagination and an active spiritual preoccupation are available to her. New ideas are formed within her head. She creates the future world; she becomes the muse.

Fourfold in the Etheric Body

Color	Quality	Element	Flow	Physical Pole	Force Flow
red	warmth	fire	centrifugal	male genital	female head pole (CNS)
yellow	light	air	centrifugal	male genital	female head pole (CNS)
green	tone/chemical	water	centripetal	female genital	male head pole
blue	life	mineral	centripetal	female genital	male head pole

By contrast, male thought processes precipitate access to free-flowing chemical and life ethers. Throughout human evolution, male pride has been a component of science. Knowledge is second nature in the soul of a man. Being scientific, a man gathers factual elements of knowledge. Through this embracing function present in the head, he gathers innumerable individual phenomena from the external world.* Such knowledge is receptive and not creative.

In the biography of each one of us the male and female realities need to be understood, be respected, and enable us to reach out to each other. The synthesis of the masculine and feminine etheric forces is the ultimate act in the recognition of the divine nature of human beings and creation and, by uniting these etheric forces concentrated in the upper pole for spiritual action and in the lower pole for reproduction, cosmic union can be attained, giving humanity the strength and joy to create. *This also leads to understanding the fact that humanity will eventually shed gender distinctions, becoming naturally androgynous again.*

---

* See, for example, Darwin, *The Voyage of the Beagle*, 1893.

Sex, Love, and the Future of Humanity

Sexuality means being sexual, which in turn has several meanings, from "having sex" to merging of male and female germ cells, not to mention the personal values we attach to these words, inspired by thoughts, fantasies, memories, and desires. In other words, *sexuality* is a simple word that means a lot to us. Compared to the amount of time we dedicate each day to our job, childcare, and recreation, the time we are actually sexual (here, meaning having sex) is relatively little. Few days pass, however, that we do not have thoughts, fantasies, feelings, or wishes that feature sex. Sexuality, eroticism, and its derivative, pornography, pervade our existence deeply enough that it justifies asking: What does sexuality mean to me? And what do I want to do with it?

One thing is clear: sexuality and love seem to be related. Then, what is love? Plato remarked that the more we know, the less we understand. That certainly seems to be the case with love. Rudolf Steiner pointed out that human beings are spirit, and that our world is the world of spiritual beings, directing us toward the insight that, if we overcome thought forms that limit the content of our thinking to the sense-perceptible world, we will graduate to perceiving beings that our eyes, ears, touch, and smell cannot discern.* Steiner speaks of angelic beings—hierarchies from Angels to Seraphim. Awareness of those beings brings us closer to understanding the future of humanity, bringing to the realms of the angelic beings qualities that only humans are able to develop. Conscious evolution of the human ability to love is intimately related to that future. Life offers many opportunities through which we can hone our ability to love freely and willingly. Sexuality is clearly one such opportunity.

To understand this, we can look more closely at what actually takes place when we have sex—or, better, make love. The German psychiatrist Wilhelm Reich, MD (1897–1957), who later in his life lived in the United States, extensively studied the

---

* See, for example, Steiner, *Anthroposophical Leading Thoughts*, pp. 37–46; also, Unger, *Language of the Consciousness Soul*, pp. 117–120.

psychophysiological basis of coitus. In the 1920s, he developed his idea of the "orgasm reflex" as the process of coitus between two people, following an energy cycle of stimulation and orgasmic relief—excitation and building tension followed by a sudden release, the orgasm, and then relaxation. It was his understanding that this cycle is a natural and rhythmically reoccurring life process, inherent to the human organization.

Plate 90: Gender differentiation in the pattern of arousal

In the arousal pattern, there is a distinct difference between the female and male. The living physiology that Spiritual Science provides recognizes the subtler bodies and their function and relationship with the elements of water, air, and fire. The divergence in the response to sexual stimulation can be experienced as a pathway through these bodies (physical body, etheric body, astral body, and the "I"). Male stimulation is often physical insofar as it has an immediate effect on the genital tissue. The erectile response does not necessarily mean that the male is ready for intimate sexual act. Reaching out to his partner, who experiences another pathway toward readiness, is an integral part of foreplay. The feminine response follows a different path; meeting someone who is on the same wavelength with her stimulates her "I." This state is followed by an active fantasy whereby her pleasure in touching and sharing herself with a partner arises from her astral body. An intensification of the play causes her to have a response of her etheric body (lubrication), which finally results in readiness for penetration. The male partner has participated in his partner's process through patience and responsiveness and experiences a heightened excitement through his etheric body and his astral body, an excitation that goes far beyond mere physical acting out.

We recognize that the life process of orgasm is only one aspect of making love. Granted, our urge to have sex arises from our physiological organization. The actual act, however, can bring us into an enormously intimate encounter with the "I," the unique, eternal being of our partner. It is the "I" in both partners that actually directs the course of the sexual act, guiding feelings of affection and tenderness and a sense of trust toward the other as the sexual tension builds. No contradictory impulses exist toward the heights of this cascading process of mutual approach between two partners.

Consciousness is turned toward the flowing sensations of pleasure—sensations that are distinctly different for male and female. She is absorbed in the preparation to receive and embrace the male;

he loses himself in her welcoming warmth as he penetrates. Then, as the involuntary orgasm approaches, the lovers lose all interest in their surroundings, absorbed as they are in their own sensations and those of the partner. The orgasm produces a loss of consciousness of one's surroundings, creating the state in which the lovers can meet each other in their true form—not perceptible to the senses. It is in this moment, when the two lovers meet in the timeless space created by the release, that we can receive our partner in the temple of our heart.

Here, then, an act of love takes place, enacted through free choice, enabling one's partner, who feels loved, to thrive in earthly life. The sexual cycle has delivered us onto a plane where we can choose time and again to open up our hearts for the "I" of the partner, making a home for this "I" in our own being. Then, relaxed, we compose ourselves, thrilled by the experience, and slowly regain awareness of life around us. Finally, we walk away from the scene, inspired to recognize in our partner, as daily life shrouds one's pure self, the "I" toward which our love flows.

An evaluation of my own gender placement in the foreign society in which I became totally assimilated permits me to question the role I occupied in this rural area. Have I, as a mother, teacher, and professional in this society, tried to share my best with the female children born in the latter part of the twentieth century? What example have I demonstrated to young women that they can beneficially emulate? How deep is the anger toward the male gender of humanity and vice versa? Am I doing the child a favor by assigning masculine or feminine connotations to social activities? Could one trace a correlation between failed partnerships while in the role of parents to this deep-seated mistrust and anger? These questions are collective, born out of the uncertainties of the times. To know who I am in my own being can help others. Willing to share these intimate life issues, I have written essays on the following subjects.

Being a Woman

Shortly after my thirteenth birthday I started to become aware of my body. Not just concerns about not always feeling well and energetic, but also joy and awe in the changes that inaugurated a new phase in my life, the ripening into womanhood. Discovering hair growth in intimate places, and later the first menses were also occasions for a personal celebration. It was empowering to realize that the designation of *woman* made me a part of a sisterhood, and I shared a special gift of reproduction. After all I was exposed to cultural mores in a restricted schooling and society of the late 1940s, a milieu in which intellectual development played a major role. Motherhood was believed to be restrictive and a sacrifice. Study came first.

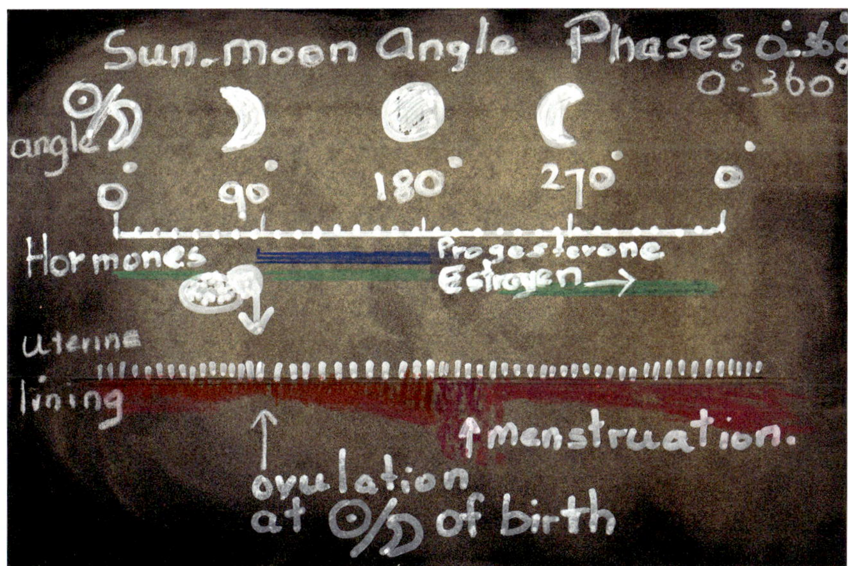

Plate 91: Three phases of hormonal secretion

In my search for an identity as a child, there was an aching antipathy toward my small female body. Hovering around me were feelings of deficiency and hopelessness in being unable to affect the world as a man could. Having an assertive disposition, being teased was unavoidable and reminded that such behavior is unacceptable in a female. Once I was inaugurated by the natural process of ripening, my body became a part of nature, submitting like clockwork to the inner lunar rhythm. Emotional instability, bodily discomfort, and restrictive activity became stumbling blocks in my life. It is through the acceptance and understanding of these hurdles that womanhood can become a distinct, affirmative aspect in one's life to explore.

To prepare the uterus for receiving the fruit of conception, there is a fluctuation in hormone levels throughout the monthly cycle. This means that a woman accedes to experiences that are foreign to her male counterpart. The presence of the ovarian hormones estrogen and progesterone and changes in the levels of these two throughout the cycle create different somatic symptoms and psychological conditions. The target for these occurring changes is the uterus. Three distinct phases within the monthly cycle can be discerned.

In the Estrogen phase after menses, the building-up of the uterine lining begins as preparation for the implantation of the fertilized egg. I would declare the time after menses as a pure state, experiencing myself balanced between the two polar excesses I still had to face in this cycle. I am free from bodily interferences. At this time only the hormone estrogen is produced, mainly by the ovary, and its circulation in my body influences the decision-making process. The effect of this hormone on my feeling life is decisive. I feel comfortable in a state of planning. I seek validation as a compassionate being, reaching out to the sick and tortured. I feel misapprehended and lost when surrounded by the hateful attitudes produced by the male hormone (testosterone) and consequent human behavior. Voicing concerns for the child, the poor, and the weak and indisposed is a social response to my interior biological nature. I become an effective voice for downtrodden humanity.

In the next phase, estrus has taken place. The ovary releases the ovum, and the dome of the cyst closes. The second hormone, progesterone, is excreted by the remnant cystic cavity. These two hormones, estrogen and progesterone, circulate through my body and change my disposition. I am influenced by warming, smoldering, fire-like energy that renders me receptive and introspective. My body starts to accumulate fluids, and awareness of the breasts and pelvic organs dominate the consciousness. I can interpret this phase as carrying an axis within myself, an imaginary median presence of fecundity reflected in the area over my heart and breasts down to the navel area and radiating into the pelvic and vulva area. The lusciousness of my being creates a social geniality that invites others to partake in my overabundance. I can woo my partner with my openness and receptiveness. In social life, I become the hostess. At my work, I can arbitrate and intercede when a crisis exists. I can solve problems using my feminine wile. This is the strength of the lower pole in the genital axis drawing of the three phases

In the third phase, both hormones stop being produced for a few days, resulting in the uterine lining breaking down and its expulsion. If an unfertilized egg is present, it is also discarded. Menstrual bleeding provides the female body with an opportunity to purify the blood, the reason a woman might be called "unclean" during this period. In this phase of low hormone levels, profound psychological changes overpower me. This is the time when, with friends or colleagues, I experience the capacity for intense philosophical conversations, brilliantly illuminated thought processes, and an amazing quality for understanding the evolving human condition. This is the strength of the upper pole of the genital axis. In the monthly cycle,

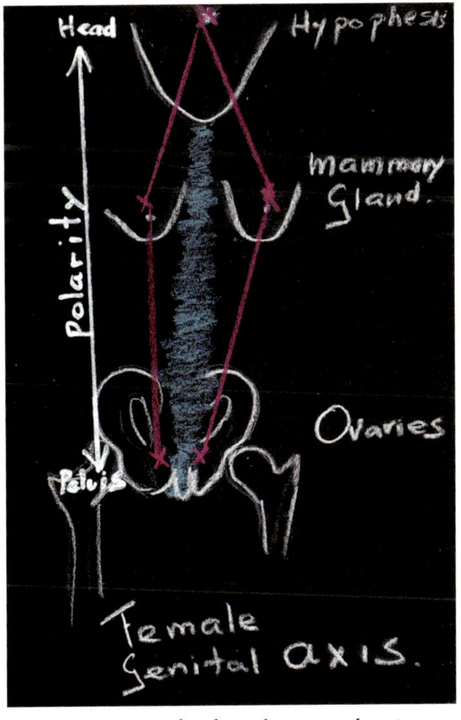

Plate 92: The female genital axis

this experience becomes a gift to me and creates a yearning for an indefinite continuation. When the physiological response of hosting a new life has failed, the individuality witnesses a profound source of moral inspiration available to her.

Within me I carry this genital axis—the axis of Love. The upper pole, the mammary glands, is shadowed by the upper arms capable of both embracing and warding off what comes toward me. This pole also embodies the head organization, with the capacity for clear thinking and creating moral thought. The lower pole is found between the mighty thighs. These pillars of strength surround the vulnerable feminine entrance and protect it from attacks and violation.

The mighty temple of Luxor was built four thousand years ago, during the time of a flourishing Egyptian civilization. This temple has also been presented as the image of the human body.* During a visit to Egypt in 1993, extraordinary experiences fructified my imagination. The Holy of Holies, the inner sanctum in the back of the hall, surrounded by strong pillars, reminded me of the feminine anatomy. Imagine rich curtain hangings representing the outer aspects of the genital anatomy, the vulva and vagina, protecting the small entry door, through which only the High Priest was permitted to enter on specific days of the year. The area was shrouded in secrecy, though I am convinced that fecundity and the invitation of descending spirit beings into the population was an essential part of a cult. A small room adjacent to the inner room is occupied with representations of the pharaoh, with an enormous phallic structure placed over the navel. Out of this organ, an abundant ejaculate flows forth. In those times, the soul of humanity was in need of direction from a theocracy. The priests directed the male population regarding humanization of the sexual act. Those were the times shortly after priestesses were replaced by masculine power. Was the time for the prominent female role in the evolution closed? Did the woman respond to her own biological physiology?

* Schwaller de Lubitz, *The Temple in Man.*

Once the productive phase ends (menopause), the ovaries start to atrophy and hormone levels diminish, it is time for enormous adjustments. Withering of the female endocrine organ in the body is experienced as waves of pouring out bodily heat followed by profound perspiration. How can these discomforts assist me in the next phase of my life? If I do not reject this phenomenon but welcome each "flush" I can cultivate the organization of my own warmth. Radiating warmth heals the ailing me so that I can find a way to stimulate social wisdom and compensate for the rejection I encounter in the society around me.

When young, using these different windows of experiences delivered to me by my internal hormonal system and the genital organs became a huge advantage in understanding the human being as we evolve toward love and freedom. As a woman, I have an opportunity to experience many talents within me that can benefit a society faced with cataclysmic changes. As I enter the crone phase wisdom develops by leaps and bounds. I dare to follow my heart and attend to latent capacities. I continue to grow.

There is a correlation between the feminine represented in humanity and in the universe. Take heed and listen! Gaya, our beloved Earth, is wounded. Her body is scarred by the craters of wars. Her breathing is impaired through deforestation. Nature, her garment, is torn and tattered. The final blow is the dictum "Axis of Evil," created politically in an act of denial that Gaya even exists. As a human proclamation and judgment, evil parts our beloved Earth, home to billions of people. Humanity can respond only by waking up to defend and protect her. As humanity, the collective feminine and masculine, we must respond with the opposite impulse, compassion, creating in our hearts an "Axis of Love," becoming One.

Isn't the Statue of Liberty a splendid example of Gaya leading us toward a promising future? She recites! America, the country in the West, becomes a haven for all. No, not foreigners, but the light for future humanity.

Give me your tired, your poor,
Your huddled masses yearning to breathe free,
The wretched refuse of your teeming shore.
Send these, the homeless, tempest-tossed to me.
I lift my lamp beside the golden door!

Being a Mother

In the expansion of infinite time and space, the human spirit **The One** incarnates on the Earth repeatedly in a process of evolving and purification to ultimately attain perfection. The choice of gender—female or male—is connected to the previous gender-defined incarnation. If the pendulum of the male incarnation has swung too far out—for example, male dominated actions that prove to be hurtful for himself or to others—the consequences for future sojourns on Earth must clearly include an incarnation in which the roles are reversed, and a vulnerable female life may be the result.

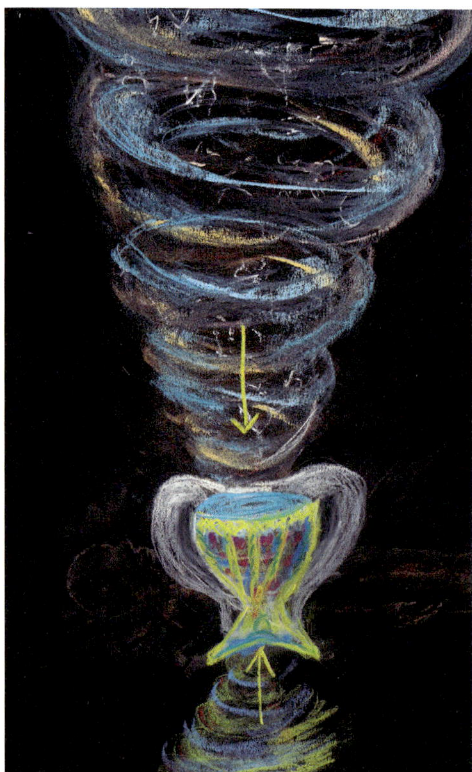

Plate 93: Female pelvis as Grail with double vortex

By design, the body of the human female carries the possibility of inviting the incoming spirit present in the surrounding cosmos to spiral down into the deepest recesses of her body, the pelvis. Two distinct round bowl formations are found in the human skeleton. One is the skull, which rounds off the height of the upright human being; the other is the pelvis, which carries the weight of the internal organs. This roundness reaches perfection only in the female pelvis. We can liken an image of this structure to a Grail for the incoming cosmic spirit, the unborn child, **The One**.

Not all female incarnations are given the opportunity of carrying a child into the world, and it's reasonable that I begin to ask myself as a woman: How can such a task become a blessing or a curse? A young woman becomes conscious that every month, again and again, her reproductive system opens to the invitation and fulfillment of a primary function of her body. Serious consideration must be given to the yearning for holding a small and vulnerable one in her arms, to augment her loneliness with another being she can call her own, or the desire to become an adult and find value in her function of motherhood.

There are so many subjective reasons why a young female might plan motherhood. Planning parenting without considering the incoming spirit being, however, is irresponsible and thus unacceptable. As parents we do not own the child; this means the child is not our possession, our play toy, or an object for acting out our own frustrations and desires. This being, **The One**, comes to the Earth to find dignity of and protection for its individuality. The ear of the mother is turned to the voice of the being that will come through her. She may hear or see it in a dream months before conception. How many times have I heard the story that the child announced itself in urgent pleas to open the door for its entry? It seems that even the father's role is delegated not as a parental donor but by the incoming **One** from a different dimension. Like lightning, the conception can have an effect on the parents-to-be. Many parents can corroborate that the hour of conception was very special for them. Through the pregnancy, the woman experiences the wonder of a new life, the growth, the movement, and the opportunity for silent but intimate conversations she holds with this new being.

Personally, my pregnancy was one of the most authentic physical experiences of my life. I had embraced the idea since the age of fourteen. Being occupied with study and later with an active professional life, not much time or inclination was given on sexual matters. During my studies in South Africa, the male fellows assigned very little sexual appeal to the female students, and this inferior portrayal continued to haunt me.

Eighteen months before the conception, while still in the Netherlands, I had a dream. I was walking down the street of my childhood home, exactly where I had a clairaudient experience as a five-year-old child. There before me stood an old fashioned pram with the hood toward me. In a slow movement, I looked around the hood and there was an adorable little boy smiling and looking at me, saying, "Make haste; I need to come!" So how is an unmarried woman, not in a relationship and on the verge of emigrating to a new country, supposed to react to such a request? I realize now that "the word of God," even at that time, was of great value to me. In my will, I was obedient to an inner voice. Could I expect such decisive ruling from above to have sensitivity for social mores of decency? In those years women were not supposed to act independently on issues of motherhood, and a child out of wedlock was unacceptable.

Nevertheless, I continued with the itinerary I had set for myself and waited, full of confidence, for the next step. In time, a revelation was imparted. The first year of residency in internal medicine was completed. America was great, and I had fully acclimatized to the people, the work, and the customs. I had purchased a new car, was moving into an apartment in Brooklyn Heights, and I anticipated a second year of residency in a large, well-known hospital. On my first visit to the hospital a few days before beginning work, the physicians were all invited to meet one another.

Even now, I can clearly reconstruct the following incident. I walk through the door, and in the front near the window a mature resident with a distinct accent (as we all had) explains the schedule.

I observe him silently, somewhat confused by the many new impressions, and I hear the following statement within: *He will be the father of your child.* I was overwhelmed, mostly with disbelief and the fact that, here again, I had no say or control over the situation. But mark my words, this is how "it" works! Human beings on the horizontal plane, if they are in the service of higher beings, will obey decisions incomprehensible to our presently limited soul life. The only dialogue that ensued was a shoulder shrug later that evening and the question: How?

To make a long story short, this person, who was the head resident, serious and pious and exceedingly attractive pursued *me* of all people. He was my type! In spite of using contraception, the entry of "my" child was secured during our first contact. I was now assigned the role of motherhood without being conscious of the vast life changes that were set into motion.

All foreign students have to pass a flex-exam to obtain a medical license and to open an independent practice in the United States. The first opportunity to do so was in September of my second year of residency. It was a four-day multiple-choice ordeal, and I had not done much preparation. So it was a surprise to receive passing results just one day after discovering my pregnancy. Now I could stay in this welcoming country and secure a "home" for this new being. I had to fight for the unborn life, because the male partner was realistic in his evaluation that a pregnancy would be an enormous burden to him as well. Not wanting to demand anything further from him, I felt strong enough to "do it alone."

With no family or close friends nearby, my situation was a complete secret. However, there was help, of course; the decisions I made were clear and concise, and each step taken toward the future always led to an improvement. I left the position as resident and moonlighted as an emergency-room physician, which I could do with the license I had secured. I found a pleasant house to share in Astoria with the most lovely elderly couple to hover over me. I felt continuously blessed.

My son (I knew it would be a male child) made every day of the pregnancy an unforgettable experience. On the day of the birth, my father was present, having made the long journey from South Africa. I fought for a natural childbirth, unheard of at that time. Breastfeeding, a natural instinctive way to succor the baby, was discouraged. For three days, we lived a restrained existence in a separate hospital room. Once discharged, the care of the child stood at the center of my life, and I could fulfill the role I had always dreamed about, not expecting it would be granted. It is the being of the child I have to thank, for its willingness to enrich my life with such an opportunity. Such a thought may sound foreign to many, but the mood of this unconditional sharing, the emotional intimate caring the mother experiences, and the whole absorption with another being, enriches the feeling life for one's whole lifetime. Of course many mothers go through this role but, as a human being's consciousness evolves, it becomes more poignant and meaningful.

The spirit of the incoming being soaring down on beams of light,
created by the intimate love existing between the parents,
to find a resting place in the deepest, most secret part of the mother.

For me, motherhood was an essential phase in my growth, a choice of the female incarnation that was fully in keeping with my destiny. Through the birthing process, I learned as woman to listen to the child's footprint on Earth. As a woman, through breastfeeding I experienced gratification in suckling and attending the innocent. Watching the first footsteps, as a woman I was reminded that the incoming being must establish independence. In attending to the child's development, I as woman must forfeit my own needs. It is inconceivable to most young parents that the incoming being also makes choices—choices of time and space, family connections, and connections with old friends.

I encourage young parents to live for a moment with the image. The image is so profound that it must have an impact on a female incarnation. Just turn to the child and say, "Thank you for choosing me, for teaching me what selflessness is, and for allowing me to experience unconditional love." As we embrace this being for a longer period of time, nurturing it and witnessing its footprints on Earth, the list for appreciation grows.

In the evolution of a human being, the earthly incarnations are essential for the development into divine being-ness. The tasks assigned to me through motherhood often seemed insurmountable. There was pain because of plans and aspirations made for the child having gone astray. How can a mother embrace actions of a child that are not acceptable in a society? We can all agree that the burden of motherhood is one of the most far-reaching and altering states in the life of a woman. It is the state of motherhood that is most exalted, but also the most misunderstood.

Chosen by **The One** for its incarnation, it creates an intimate association between two human beings regardless of gender. Did it exist before? It surely will result in the continuation of a bond between two beings that is infinite and intimate on a soul level. The first son especially can become a light being for the mother. This could become misconstrued as the overt bonding as we can witness with dominating behavior of one person over another. Pathological relationships are nurtured by the insecurity and unhappiness of an unenlightened mother figure. Through the support of a strong family structure, such situations can be recognized and prevented.

The Act of Marriage

The wedding feast is a celebration that draws people together in joy and communion throughout the world. As an institution, it is sanctified before the community in a ceremony, usually in a religious setting. It is legalized through the courts of law and today gives the partners advocacy for each other regardless of the sexual orientation. The merging of bride and bridegroom as one stirs a deep-seated promise that human beings are not meant to be alone during our sojourn on Earth. Marriage must have a spiritual connotation, but the true meaning of this institution has eluded humanity. Contemplating the full meaning of the bond between two people, a life-affirming bond that also entices **The One** to merge, reaches beyond subjective experience. Monogamy is strictly a subjective choice for both partners in a sexual relationship not destined for reproductive purposes. Why? Physical attraction between two persons is a spontaneous phenomenon, short lived, and without a foundation built on trust. Pure lust for the enjoyment for each other is born from a self-centered need and fulfills the purpose for that moment. Personal freedom is preserved and there are no promises for the future.

In the medical therapeutic field it is recognized that a spontaneous orgasmic reflex is part of a physiological response mechanism. The sexual act for one or both partners can bring an orgasmic release. Onanism, though forbidden by fundamentalist religious orders, is practiced with joy and dedication by both sexes. For the past fifty years, pornography has been readily available on the Internet and has become a part of this cycle. It finds a fecund soil with the generation of those who have lost their own powers of imagination and have become addicted to the world of virtual reality. Explicit reenactments created by producers without scruples, who live in and through these sordid activities, remain lucrative and rewarding. In that world there is no room for subtlety.

The wedding, in contrast to the marriage, could be a joyous ceremony in a community, to recognize and support the intent of a couple in the interaction with each other on all levels. For older couples beyond the reproductive years, such a partnership is constructive, supportive, and includes loving care during the years of aging.

There is the reality, in the process of evolution, that embraces the concept of "holy" partnership. Increasingly, human beings have a desire to begin a "loving" partnership with a like-minded person who can be trusted and accepted. The practice of placing the other one before my own selfish tendencies becomes the challenge in such a relationship. Trust is needed, because both partners desire to live for, with, and in each other. Such a liaison places the human child, **The One**, on a pathway of maturation, embracing a potential for growth and learning personally the concept of unconditional love. Can anyone imagine what such a path would look like? Here are two human beings, walking hand in hand, physically attracted to each other, each in the process of dedicating all efforts to the growth of the other, weaving their destiny in a functional foundation to contribute to a society that surrounds them. The necessity of tuning into the conversation of each other is recognized by both partners, and one offers space for the emotions of the other. One's own needs are clearly defined and one is in tune with the needs of the other. A tapestry is woven in this way, one in which the threads of different colors create a unique cloth and even a garment for a new entity or idea to join this small but strong family.

Marriage becomes a necessity only for the protection of the incarnating spirit being. Into the group of two, a third party is invited and consciously allowed to enter. It is in this mood of desire from both parents and a deep reverence for the procreation of a new earthly body that such a process can be initiated. The commitment to **The One** lasts as long as it takes for the young being to mature (twenty-one years).

Humanity is learning about love and is active in the process of evolving toward perfection. Studying the New Testament may bring me on a path of recognition that the protagonist, the figure of the baptized Jesus, was the Son of God. This supreme lofty being became the incarnation of *Love*. He is likened to the bridegroom, choosing as His partner collective humanity (the soul of humanity, *Gaya*) in its potential as spirit beings. In the future, a wedding can be expected between the bride (humanity) and the bridegroom (the Christ-being) so that the metamorphosis into Godhood can be vouchsafed.

As Lover

There are invariable ways that I can move my love.
It is not in what I do, but in being pure and spontaneous,
an overflow of my deep love for his nearness,
his warmth and his ability to give so unconditionally.
I cannot fathom what goes in his mind, the power of his being,
and yet the little hesitation in his breath tells me
of his complete captivation with something new to him.
The softness of his soul must frighten him,
out of control indeed he could get hurt.

But beloved, I give myself to you,
so that you can explore my being.
I need to be moved by you
moved by your tenderness,
eagerness to discover ever more
the variables you have kindled.
So it is the you and the me
reaching out to touch
that which is Eternal,
Love everlasting.

The Credo

For most people, religious affiliations are kept private and somewhat obscure. To be associated professionally with an "evangelical" organization states not necessarily that "we are better" but acknowledgment of a spiritual world (vertical plane) and a personal belief system. Strangely enough, for disciples of Christianity, many twists and turns exist, enabling in one's faith to have human views that lead to strife and dissent.

Stories of personal faith, much like our bed or bathroom habits, are so intimate that even with longtime friends, customs such as prayer, meditation, and reactions to subjective beliefs are often not discussed or even revealed. So I was surprised when I saw a recent newspaper article in which a "confession of faith" questionnaire was discussed. The poll concluded that only in the state of Mississippi were more than sixty percent of the citizens able to discuss their faithfulness to a Christian conviction openly and with enthusiasm. This provoked my own questions surrounding authenticity and how the meaning of my own life could be expressed as a unique testimony, not of success but a testimony of my continuing work in progress toward a moral imagination true to my personal "confession of faith."

The Apostolic Creed is recited by members of the Community of Christ, regardless of denomination. Mostly, this has become rote lip service that asks to be replaced by a bold individual conviction. As the conscious soul awakens in an evolutionary process of spiritual growth, the "I" of the human being, **The One**, must be enabled and provoked to stand before humanity and state a personal conviction, "What I live by." Such an exercise may be difficult for younger people, but it is interesting that the younger generation of nineteenth-century Europe, having been earmarked as privileged aristocracy, were encouraged to create such a Credo during their twenties. Those Credos may be found in historical contexts and in the biographies of prominent individuals (usually male) who lead empires and civilizations. What are the considerations in fashioning such a document?

1. To be free of the influence of educational institutions, and with the desire to test everything through experience
2. To know with certainty and inner conviction: Divine revelation exists; one can peruse the vertical plane
3. To place a value of self within a social context: one's place on the horizontal plane and personal impact through one's work.
4. Placing oneself in time and space and infinity
5. Am I loved? My desires in connection with the question: Can I experience Love?

A Credo emerges from a human being in search of Self at a time in one's biography when "I" starts to manifest (years 21 to 28). The creation of such a document might be seen as a selfish preoccupation, but one realizes at a later age or at the end of one's life that revisions are made when that statement is made as an expression of conscious soul experience. One's credo, in a figurative sense, can form impenetrable boundaries around it and does not necessarily need to be shared with anyone else.

Being a Doctor

In reviewing my life, it has become clear that my destiny was intimately connected with the medical discipline and, as luck would have it, during the unfolding of my biography I was postured with one foot on the African continent—where the witch doctor (*sangoma*) was still common in rural areas of South Africa—and the other foot in the Western medical mode and indoctrinated into the materialistic mechanical-scientific discipline that is modern natural science. At the end of the 1950s, one's knowledge was still tested orally with professors; written questions tested us on both quantitative and qualitative levels of scientific inquiries and our teachers still carried their own studies and interests into the curriculum.

Once I was situated as an independent voice in my role as a rural physician, it became clear that the threat of change, as the Sword of Damocles, hung over most physicians. Aspects of healthcare touted as essential to the future were listed as follows: protect yourself (CYOA) through expensive insurance from the litigation of dissatisfied patients and their families. With the increasing emergence of insured patients, contracts are made between insurance companies and healthcare providers, while independent physicians are largely ignored. Large group practices with ten or more physicians were encouraged to sign up. The result is that the unique patient-doctor relationships are endangered. Most physicians are content to become a mere cog in the wheel of today's system of medical delivery, commonly called the "healthcare industry."

This was also the time when the pharmaceutical companies desired greater power over decisions of treatment protocols. A subtle power play between the insurance companies and the pharmaceutical companies made it mandatory under the guise of "preventive medicine" to immunize all children and, later, to use certain medications in patient groups of the practices the insurance companies had secured. The reality was that doctor-patient information was no longer confidential. Who made these incisive decisions—pencil pushers or medical professionals?

Diagnostic accuracy was increasingly delegated to the mechanical diagnostic equipment of hospitals and group practices. Once an expensive diagnostic tool is installed, many more patients have to undergo testing to defray the costs of the machines. I remember clearly one wise colleague making exactly that point during a staff meeting at our local hospital. The staff was being consulted on the acquisition of an MRI (magnetic resonance imaging) machine, costing more than a million dollars. He remarked, "Once the machine is installed, patients will be lined up to undergo the procedure." These are just some of the factors contributing to the skyrocketing cost of so-called healthcare today.

During the years I practiced in this county, I was privileged to remain independent from insurance companies, which guaranteed office confidentiality and a medical practice whereby my patients themselves would reimburse me for the time I spent with them during consultations.

Arrows pierced my heart as I realized that the future medical model would be mechanistic. The human spirit and life quality, dignity and personal biography are no longer given attention or even recognized. The physician's time and willingness to be authentic and interested are necessary. As a physician, I submit that all encounters will change me For such a relationship between the physician and the person who seeks advice to take place, . I am molded, I am transformed, and I am used. How can these sacrificial qualities be inculcated into the training of young physicians?

The concept of healing as a living science requires healers with moral imagination, and this is dying out and foreign to Western medical education. Moral imagination as an individual strength is introduced here. This capacity requires aspiring young physicians to become familiar with inner silence, resting the overactive mind that constantly reviews. Inner silence enables the enlivening of imagination, which draws a picture of the patient with an illness and digests the pathology that is presented not just as a mechanical failure but also taking into consideration the patient's biography, a thorough background of the individual.

Does the solution come immediately, like a wind? Wisely, we can say we'll sleep on it, and in the morning we remember that even at night we, as physicians, have undergone a correction for the patient's healing. I realize that I, the physician, can heal nothing without the help of a qualitative entity related to unknown factors we can call *Grace*, as well as the patient's will to heal through me.

During the silence when practicing living imagination with a patient, thinking becomes an activity: "It thinks in me." The method of healing is revealed: how we speak, what remedy to use, what test to order. The goal is to alleviate suffering. We evoke the activity of inspiration through the soul function of reasoning, weighing opposites, and picturing the parameters of a living process, which contributes to a conscious evaluation. This is living thinking. This medical discipline, aided by Spiritual Science, cannot be imagined in a culture steeped in the materialistic worldview of natural science.

Successful students present unique capacities, the most highly praised of which is memory, assertive decisiveness, and a mathematical thought process. Individuals with strong ideals and "moral" values can barely come to terms with such demands. Personal attitudes have no place in training medical students who are influenced by pharmaceutical manipulation and technological diagnostic methods. The subjective becomes objective by teaching and indoctrination of natural scientific principles.

Expressions of knowledge continue along the horizontal materialistic plane in which time is finite and death is the ultimate demise of life. Collectively, humanity loves a long life on Earth, abhors death and suffering, and rejects solitary existence, and natural science will continue to offer solutions to these facts of life. The curriculum of medical study in the West focuses on knowledge and memory of natural scientific facts, information that is reproducible and tested through multiple-choice questions. The student's imagination is stimulated through visual images and text on computer screens, and virtual reality threatens to become the imagination of the future. Living thought processes that challenge the opinions of students are considered too time-consuming and are unpopular in most institutions of higher learning.

We need to remember that a few students of all ages are still interested in exploring suprasensory phenomena and their consequent impact on human evolution, and we still have the freedom to examine such avenues. Consideration of the spiritual dimensions of our fellow human beings' needs and developing the art of listening are essential tools in fully comprehending patients and their needs. If such discerning practitioners are discouraged in exploring the nature of the whole human being, true healing modalities will not evolve. Future education must encompass the full inheritance of a reincarnating entity, the commonalities between human nature and the cosmos, and realizing that there is more to life than our visible horizontal reality. Natural science must be augmented with a science of the spirit. Otherwise, we negatively influence our own return to a future life of freedom.

The dangers of the current medical mode we are dealing with must be recognized. The modalities of diagnostic tools, pharmaceutical intervention, and mechanical surgical corrections have become pillars of medical triage and form the guidelines for modern conventional healthcare. If something is wrong with the body, we will correct it. Continuation of these practices obfuscates the role of the *healer*. Most physicians today are willing to forgo the title, the honor, the respect, the distinction, and so on, so long as they are well paid. Hasn't the intimate title "healer" proven to be an old-fashioned concept today for students emerging from universities with medical degrees?

Medicine is an art as long as it remains recognized as such. In the Germanic-speaking countries, to receive a medical degree makes a statement that "I have become a practitioner in the *art* of medicine." This does not carry a title "doctor." That title should be earned through rigorous university training and a thesis after earning a master's degree. The title "doctor" indicates educational leadership to those pupils coming after.

To practice the *art* of medicine and healing, I resort to what I know from my own being-ness—authenticity, individualized treatment as a reflection of my "thinking about," and an urge to experience a subjective solution to "healing the other." When a work of art is displayed in a museum, people come to see it because it radiates beauty and uplifts the viewer; it radiates healing power. When a patient and a physician sit together searching for a solution to an imbalance experienced as an illness, unseen powers flowing from both individuals and family play a role in their exchange. A time element is introduced into the interaction. It takes time and an intimate environment for a process of enlightened exchange to occur. One's visit to a "doctor" must include the qualities of listening, silence, and compassion. It becomes possible, then, that the circle of such an exchange widens to encompass many impulses and beings. Insight into "the other" arises from sources of inspiration and intuition. In truth, a physician can never claim the "healing." Modesty and integrity become second nature to the healer. One emulates the exemplary life of a true alchemist, who could still claim, "Change and be changed!"

Requesting a chair in a medical college named "Life Philosophy" would be refreshing. We recognize this in Hermes Trismegistus. Not wanting to reinvent the wheel, his postulates remain valid and in the future will create the scaffolding for truth and accuracy in healing. It is immodest to make claims about the efficacy of the art in medicine extended by Anthroposophy. After all, in this practice I advocate that patients should precipitate in their healing process, and as a physician I become a guide. However, no guide can make progress unless a map is available, a clear picture of the person, including a genetic profile, as well as time and space in the biography, evaluation of the resilience of etheric forces, evaluation of the astral organization's effect on mobility and mental stability, and, last but not least, recognition of the individuality that shimmers beyond all the discoveries, just as the light of the Sun illumines our path in life. The physician must recognize and support what the patient's true individuality can identify as its aim in this earthly life. This becomes healing.

Far from just offering advice, these guidelines for each of the hundreds of patients sitting down with me have been invaluable. I am willing to share these with practitioners of future generations, young people who have submitted to the shrinking process of scientific methods, endured nights and days without respite, and survived the process. The generation before us must lead the way through their desires, dreams, creative urges, and hear the voices of encouragement.

Sound U

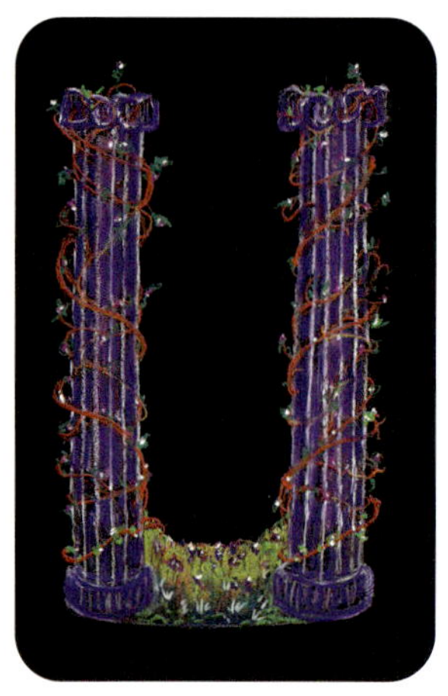

Unique, universe, ubiquitous, utopia, eulogy—all words beginning with the strong U sound. They indicate or reflect wholeness, an ideal being fulfilled. In the U experience, I arrive at the conclusion of my life. This becomes the experience of where I stand as a pillar, securing the human structure I support. Rooted steadfastly in the Earth, upright, I reach out beyond the skull, arms covering the ears, high, straight, in a parallel formation touching realms of Heaven. Who am I? Who is waiting? What will the future bring?

Subjectively, the U section of my life is very much reflected in the heavenly music of Gustav Mahler's *Das Lied von der Erde*. As the music of the final stanza softly fades, I find myself in full consciousness on the threshold of a new beginning that stretches into infinite distances. Listen!

I stand here waiting for my friend;
I wait for him to take a last farewell.
Where are you? You have left me alone so long!
Oh beauty! O world, drunk forever with love and life!
Where am I going? I shall wander in the mountains,
I am seeking rest for my lonely heart.
Still is my heart, it is awaiting its hour!

Everywhere the lovely earth blossoms forth in spring
and grows green
Anew! Everywhere forever, horizons are blue and bright!
For ever and ever.

—Gustav Mahler

It is the last song, dedicated to the poignant farewell of the Earth-dweller. I am filled with the heaviness of parting, the yearning for the loveliness of Earth's infinite cycle, birth and death and the unknown dimensions of the future. Where will I go?

In contemplating my review of what is in the past, understanding the life of my contemporaries has value. Future goodness is born in us from our accumulation of past-life experiences, now leavened by the yeast of wisdom. What was not considered before beckons with tantalizing urgency. Writing, poetry, music, literature, and research are all explorations for which time is set aside. Could one have hoped for such enrichment later in life, meeting aspects of the self that is completely foreign if not allowed the time to contemplate?

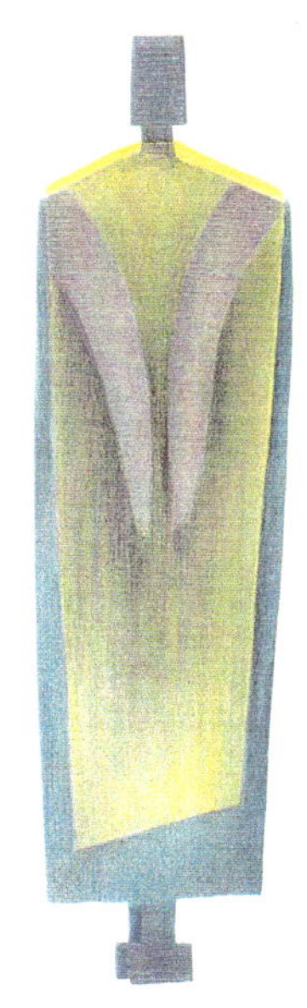

Plate 95: Eurythmy gesture of U

This section is dedicated to the review and further illustration of the ideas that have been introduced throughout this book. One repeated question concerns the fourfold organization of the human being and a request for examples. I can find these layers of activity reflected in the historic stories that collective humanity carries throughout times immemorial—myths, fairytales, fables, parables, and legends.

Myths are connected with the physical accomplishment of an individual, an outstanding feat that memorializes that man or woman. I am reminded of Joan of Arc, who in a female body accomplished such a remarkable masculine task. The myth remains hidden to us until we reach a stage of physical independence.

As children we are privy to a wealth of fairytales—stories that arise from the collective unconscious, stories rich in symbolism, stories that are simply imbibed and require no explanation. These tales fall under the heading of creations that come from the life force in all of humanity, stories connected to the ether body and common to all of us.

Fables and parables become familiar to us later in our development when, as human beings, we have a consciousness that can say, *I stand corrected—my bad!* Emotional ripening depends on the astral body and fully occupies our being-ness after sexual maturation.

It is only in legends that the individual "I" begins to weave a tapestry of its own identity on Earth. The threads can have the quality "I" choose, varying between luster and dull gray. It is the feat of individualism that we can reflect upon only after the biography is complete. An authentic review of such a life creates the legend.

In human evolution, the stories become reflections of soul as experienced on Earth, both past and present. As the human being is still a work in progress, future stories will be written that reflect the evolving godliness of humankind. What stories would those be? Tales of sacrifice, of reconciliation, of triumphs? Humanity will always accumulate and present stories. Intimate, personal, authentic reflections of life's laments and triumphs enrich the traveler during one's sojourn on Earth. We all find solace, hope, and soul in the art of storytelling and representation of images.

The Physical Organization, Myth, and the Vertical Plane

Plate 96: Life becomes a walk through a labyrinth

Each person is born and has a unique physical identity, whether a footprint or DNA, to make a claim on being part of the human family. Birth becomes a weighty proposition when we examine the physical body in the light of such an individual representation. The existence of the physical body on Earth makes possible heroic deeds to be remembered in story, song, and pictures. As the time goes by, the biography as a story assumes a mythical quality. As we learned from **The One** finding its "home" and deploying its boundaries at the moment before conception, the opportunity for a preview is extended. Still protected by the "arms of the angel," choices in gender and genetic disposition (all physical accouterments) will be chosen while the blueprint of its personal myth is viewed. The question lingers: In which physical garment can one's earthly task best be accomplished?

Consider the assignment given to Joan of Arc (1412–1431), The Maid of Orléans. At the age of 18, she played a heroic role in the Siege of Orléans, which led to subsequent victories for the French king, Charles VII, and the end in 1453 of the Hundred Year's War between England and France. Yet this individual chose the female gender born to a peasant family. Only the Angels could foresee the appropriateness of such choices.

In fulfilling its myth, **The One** considers the task for the immediate future, life on Earth, and the connection with the assignment needed for such an accomplishment. The preview, although hidden in the recesses of our unconscious, will be examined again during the process of departing from Earth. The review of life is experienced with our last breath. The availability of both suprasensory views is like two blueprints to be displayed for comparison after the physical body is left behind. There are beautiful images available in museums in which the Egyptian Pharaohs, following death, had to face the trial of weighing the heart for purity of thought and intentionality of the will. In the beginning of our life, a burning desire to accomplish is experienced, and at the end of life a consternation to find that the blueprints do not coincide. Where have we gone astray? Where did we take a wrong turn? The discrepancy between these two blueprints, the preview and the review, becomes a contributing source for the material accumulated for further review of time spent between two earthly lives. "To do it better the next time" is the sincere and hopeful greeting Cherokees express at their departure from this world.

The text in all the chapters reminds the reader that, throughout the life of **The One**, there is deep knowing that a higher order avails itself for its protection, guidance, and accomplishment of ideals. Most people are oblivious to these admonitions and even those with a religious background give scant validity to spirit, the higher self. The plane of the vertical dimension, a plane where higher powers are recognized, a plane in which **The One** can discover its interaction with "the beloved," must become accessible to all. As human beings we strive mostly for worldly goods and status and fail to review our day by asking: *Are we still on track with our ideals and most fervent desires?*

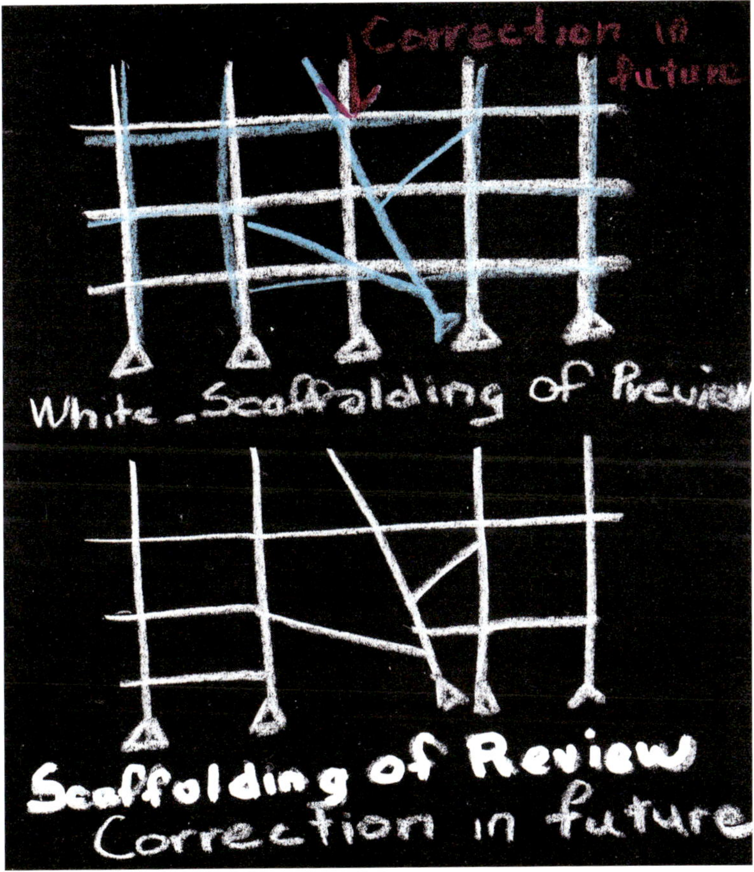

Plate 97: Preview and review

How can I share with the reader the experience of preview and review as a contribution to the imagination? Can such experiences happen randomly and anywhere? An experience such as this takes place beyond the senses but can become a percept through memory. Without involving the outer senses, one becomes immersed in pictures, voices, and even scenery, all of which are multilayered. In our dream life, such images are created and, with training, can be recalled on awaking. Playing itself out beyond the physical body, the perceiving organ is not part of or in the body and must be recognized as not bound to one dimension—vision, for instance. With hearing, we experience sound all around. The vertical plane surrounds the probing and quiet investigator and rewards it with spontaneous insights. We can call these *inspirations* and *intuitions*. The observer imprints suprasensory stimuli as memories. Unexplainable, they are nevertheless experiences that must be real.

Using the physical body allows **The One** to contemplate the marvel of its atomic structure and the lawfulness of its natural chemistry, reveling in a superior and unique upright structure while moving on Earth. The capacities beyond these gifts enable **The One** to prepare the mythical story of heroism, to reconnect the bridge between two worlds, and to dedicate itself to the evolution of the species. Most of the time, however, introducing, reviewing, and evaluating the story that each person lives on Earth can be done only at the time of death. We hear many such stories during the funerals of family, friends, and acquaintances, but mostly those lines of the eulogy are often confabulated and not authentic.

What needs to develop, of course, is the capacity to listen to one's own inner voice. No story can unfold with noise surrounding or within us. With an imagination, our own myth becomes authentic and manifests throughout life with a stubborn certainty. The story continues. The development of a personal confession of faith, also referred to as a credo, is an exercise for the individual after the age of twenty-one. This becomes a final concrete testimony of the "I." Contemplating our own essence—not what those around us want but what it is we can give—is the foundation of real growth and worth.

Etheric Organization and Fairytales

Beginning with "Once upon a time" and ending with "and they lived happily ever after" wraps the child in us in a blanket of security. These tales are repeated over and over and curiously each child has his or her favorite. This collective material, still alive in the unconscious folk soul all over the world, hardly requires the images of picture books, movies, and theme parks. The content speaks to and satisfies children on an unconscious level and is carried from generation to generation. I would say, too, that the creation of explicit virtual realities such as have been introduced into today's Western culture exploits and dulls the child's imagination.

Stories of witchcraft, supernatural beings conversing with the protagonist, and family members who act out of malice or evil intent are certainly palatable to most children and play a role in their fantasy and the world of make-believe. However, a more profound connection to the functional bodily systems can be detected, and the enactment of those stories becomes therapeutic. The question arises: Can we find a fruitful imagination between these collective stories and our bodily functions? We find it in the four organs, each with a distinct function and contribution to the body's chemical constitution. The etheric body contains the parameters of forces, and four distinct characteristics can be identified: *fire* (warmth), *light* (air), *tone* (water), and *chemistry* (minerals).

In the fairytales left to us by the Grimm Brothers, I can find specific connections with the formative forces of the organs, warmth ether, light ether, tone ether, and chemical (or life) ether. These stories began in tight communities in which elders received recognition for their "knowing" and were sought out for their wisdom. The lay person had an ear, could understand the stories woven by the older people of the community, stories weaving into their own healing powers on a deep unconscious level. The last phrase confirmed the resolution and success story.

Ending with the phrase "they lived happily ever after," the listener, usually a child, collected those images before sleep, digested them at night, and healed the wayward stalker within its own unbalanced body. Healing does not necessarily indicate a return to balance but certainly a shift from a deep hidden nature to gainful insight into a pathology so it can be worked on in daytime consciousness.

The content of fairytales can direct the "organizer" of health (the etheric body) to bring balance where there is an abundance or shortage of the warmth, light, tone or chemistry, and to "set things right" in the natural function of the body. Only then can the cells in their distinct functions together "live happily ever after." The body as an accumulation of different cells can be interpreted in this sense as a living entity, interacting together for the health and balance of the whole.

Let me introduce the wide variety of organ functions as the seed material for your own story. In daily life nothing is as personal as the habits we display over and over again. What are my habits? My bodily organization carries deep inside involuntary movements—facial tics, gestures, laughter, speech—that convey myself to the world. Habits acquired on Earth are nearly impossible to change; they are, so to speak, the signature of who I am and are a part of the etheric organization.

Like the four pillars bearing the roof of a Greek temple, the four organs of our physical body—kidney, liver, lung, and heart—fulfill their task of conveying a personal profile. Is there a link between the four organs and the habitual gestures we incorporate? Through acquaintance with the other person, whether a close family member, a friend, or a neighbor, I can identify a distinct signature in each person. On the physical level, it is our DNA that becomes unique, thousands of protein building blocks of amino acids. Such a spiral-shaped protein becomes a foothold for the formative forces specific to each of us. Individual proteins present in the body fluids are a component of the "living water" we have described. The etheric body is sometimes referred to as the *habit body*. The physical body carries the distinct chemical makeup of our DNA. The etheric body contributes to our unique habitual profile.

Plate 98: Temple with four pillars

The Liver

The four organs are a source of our habitual life. Let me explain this with the following Tale connected with the Liver and Gallbladder organs. The familiar story is as follows:

Prometheus, presented to humanity as a son of Zeus, frequently visited the Earth and sympathized with the laborious life humanity had to endure. Then, being sleepy and experiencing no fun, he endeavored to bring the arts of music, dance, and weaving of colorful cloths so that their lives could be improved. For this, Prometheus was punished, because that early awakening of the sentient soul life was against the wishes of the ruling god. For forty long years he was chained, day and night, to rocks of the Caucasus Mountains. His only companion was the Eagle that devoured his liver starting at sunrise, and with sleep at sunset the wounded liver was healed throughout the night. This circadian rhythm of the liver was hereby introduced: the bile excretion commences at sunrise (around four a.m.) for twelve hours, followed by the liver's metabolism for the next twelve hours. This circadian rhythm has become habitual for the etheric organization connected to the liver/bile organ. A constitutional weakness in the liver gallbladder system that can usually be diagnosed would cause a disturbance in these functions and open the door to pathology.

Plate 99: Facial gestures

Our habitual profile is reflected not only in the presentation of our body (*gestalt*), but also in our emotional reactions. On an emotional level, the liver/gallbladder synchronicity has a far-reaching influence on our temperaments. Are you a choleric, full of fire? Your bile is strong and the temper is close to the surface. For a melancholic, the bile is black and sticky and moves slowly. This person drags through life with a heavy mood, downcast and negative. The sanguine personality experiences life as a blast, dancing and scurrying, with many places to go but with a short attention span. The phlegmatic typifies a balanced, organized, and methodical liver type, trustworthy and steady as clockwork. We know for ourselves that temperaments cannot change. One's etheric signature remains in this life until the end of days.

The liver system is designated by the two diametrically opposed physiological functions of construction and excretion. They can be seen as a polarity, with the one pole responsible for the anabolism, a constructive process by which a cell takes the substance required for repair and growth from the blood and builds it in to a cytoplasm, thus converting a nonliving material into the living cytoplasm of the cell, typically storing energy. The other pole, catabolism (excretion), includes all the processes in which complex substances are converted into simpler substances, usually with the release of energy and excretion.

anabolism	chemical/life	endothermic	centripetal	liver
catabolism	warmth/light	exothermic	centrifugal	bile

We can wonder if here, too, the etheric organization—with its four distinct formative forces of warmth ether, light ether, chemical ether, and life ether—is not functionally designated to each of the metabolically opposed regions. The liver organ itself dominates the centripetal chemical ether and ether life forces, the forces that function as gatherers of substances and give form to living water and chyle. The bile in the ducts and the gall bladder display the centrifugal activity of the warmth ether and the light ether, with outward radiation, heightened activity influencing transmuting chemicals into waste products in a process of catabolism.

Out of this interplay between polar opposites, our personal story, the fairytale, unfolds. The liver, being such a mighty organ, shapes the personality, the fluctuation between moods of abundance or frugality, psychologically designated *mania* and *depression*. The fairytale itself often uses a gender distinction between the two lead protagonists—for instance, the bewitched sleeping princess and the traveling, courageous rescuing prince, opposite actors or forces finding balance through each other.

In mental disorders, one can attribute bipolar disorder to a liver constitution that runs in families, therefore of a genetic disposition. Here an imagination that one of the pillars of the temple (our body) is unable to carry the full load of function on its "shoulders." From this information, can I ask the reader to create a personal profile? Does the repetitive push and pull of these organs find an expression in one's own habitual presentation in life? Give self-examination a try. Can you recognize yourself in your liver function? Do you have a liver profile?

The Lung

Plate 100: Carbon

The lung organ, for its transmission of life-giving air into the blood, has a different tale to tell. Let's not look objectively from the outside at the rib cage, which protects the lung and heart so perfectly. Imagine crawling inside and having a subjective experience of the constrictive feeling of imprisonment behind the horizontal bars of the ribs. It becomes elementary that the exchange between inhaled oxygen and exhaled carbon dioxide involves the entrapment of an oxygen molecule by a carbon molecule associated with all life on Earth. Listen to its riddle:

I am an atom with greedy hand
Reaching out to many a friend
Holding on to all my brothers
Become pitch black like the others
Crushed by the heaviest of weights
Will then release the purest of lights
In the Kingdom of plants I will provide
Skeleton, structure, and scaffold aside
On Earth I make friends in flowers and fruits
Fashioning colors and patterns for suits
I marry many a bride but am loyal to none
Dancing with water gives all a spin
Bedding with nitrogen I sentence to death
Merging with oxygen gives new breath
Like a bird in the sky. I rise and set free
Life on Earth I have to flee
I organize nature, order abounds
For the created One chained to the ground
I release and set free to return to beyond.

If I am asking myself what substance defines the Earth, the answer can be found in this versatile carbon molecule. Our planet, solid earth, is constituted from a mixture of silica, aluminum, and carbon. However, an alien visitor would find an abundance of the carbon molecule throughout all substances—solid, water, and air—and conclude that on this planet the carbon molecule is an indication of life forms existing from the beginning, because carbon is connected to life and the living kingdoms as we know them.

The lung organ is utilized to bring the carbon in the air into the small alveoli, where it becomes active in the mechanism of exchanging all the solid substances suspended in the living water of the physical body. By inhaling, oxygen is supplied to the blood and the excess of carbon is exhaled. The breathing mechanism works unconsciously in a steady seesaw motion, in – out – in – out. Weakness in the organ of the chest cage affects my breathing, so that I suddenly become aware of an arrhythmic function. I heave, I pant, I sense hunger for air, I suffocate, and I am imprisoned. Like a caged bird, I am restricted in my movement and not free; I must submit to the reality of being locked up with a bag over my head. Despondency overcomes me, because I and the solidity of the Earth have become one (as in Grimms' fairytale, *Jorinda and Joringel*).

One can have a mental experience of restraint when, constitutionally, a genetic weak lung "pillar" is diagnosed. Each day, I can be confronted by anxieties that hinder me in free self-expression. Questions such as, "Have I turned off the water?" "Is the door locked?" Likewise, in an obsessive profile with phobias and compulsive tendencies, I can see myself not being free—in other words, as a *lung personality*. These personality traits are dominant through family lines and thus have a genetic character. It becomes a challenge when these personality characteristics are interpreted with a fairytale innuendo. What story could I fashion for myself and how could my tale end in "living happily ever after"?

Notice that the feminine and masculine aspects are both present in the fairytale. Carl Jung unraveled the significance of his personal psyche as a gender duality, which he named *animus* and *anima*. Did he stumble on the life activity of the formative force within himself? Didn't he find in the male who in his sexual organ is bound by the centrifugal formative forces of warmth ether and light ether, the urge to vanquish, dominate, and possess? Then, the same free radiating formative forces are present in the head pole now, as his muse, a feminine companion, his Beatrice (a soul in Dante's *Divine Comedy*).

The opposite picture can be constructed in the psyche of the female, whereby she experiences a body-bound compulsion to be dominated—water-clogged, indolent, and slow to escape, she rather submits out of her nature. Her triumph comes in the form of the prince, in shining armor, riding a white fiery steed.

Aah! These are the fantasies with which our psyche rescues us from a life of doldrums! They are symbols of people, animals, and fairies, all part of the collective memories of humanity and hidden as the formative forces of each organ. One functions in life out of the formative forces unique to each of us. This organization penetrates the solid, earthly body (the ashes). With my "death," these forces will be released into the cosmos, becoming a part of the collective memory of the world.

The Kidney

The Kidney, an organ of excretion, has again a different story. The expression "Urine is the mummy of the astral body" was left to me by my mentor in anthroposophically extended medicine, Otto Wolf, MD, a master in the art of teaching and storytelling. Leaving his pupils with such a statement guaranteed our continuous loyalty and dedication to the (still) unknown riddles the living body presents. This section is not intended to concentrate on the astral body but to look at the kidney, not only as the organ for excretion but also to search for the anabolic and the catabolic functions—the polarity.

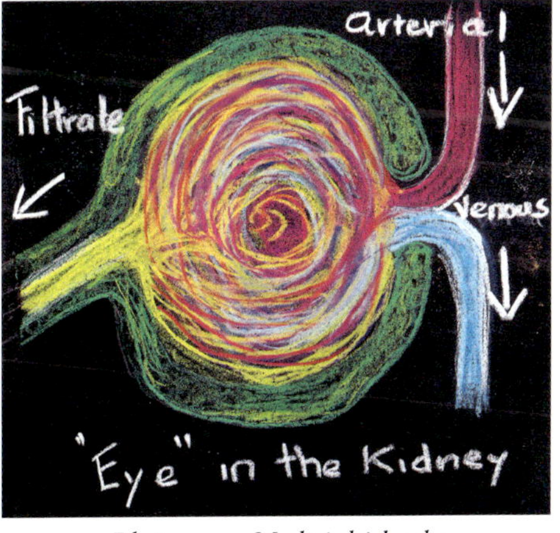

Plate 101: Malpighi body

Urine consists of dead water (95%) and solids (5%), the latter being in solution. The kidney acts to maintain homeostasis of the blood and body fluids. Physiologically, the renal system can be divided into two contrasting functions. It is certain that the anatomical kidney has to submit to constant vigilance; each drop of blood is scrutinized by a glomerular body that looks like an eye.

Why? So that I can see you better, smell you better, taste you better! *Little Red Riding Hood* contains the story of this organ, an inner sense organ.

The anabolic function of the kidney is connected to the transformation and maintenance of living water. The catabolic function results in the excretion of urine (dead water, the mummy). What is living water? The fluid body occupies ninety percent of one's total body weight. It cannot be compared to urine, blood serum, or a synthetic liquid in which all the constituents of organic and inorganic molecules are dissolved to imitate body fluid. Understanding the concept of "life," we enter the etheric organization, the world of imponderable quality. This becomes a realm where I have to divert my thinking from a nonliving concept to incorporate the living cell in its reality. This cell has the capacity to stabilize itself constantly, thanks to the etheric life forces present in every living thing. This would mean that ninety percent of our physical organism is assigned the task of maintaining the life function. It penetrates the whole bodily structure, whether asleep or awake, and has self-regulating anabolic and catabolic aspects.

From the renal system, living water irradiates the entire organization. Living water permeated by the etheric organism moves through the entire organism. The etheric organism is permeated completely by imaginations. This is important to know if I want to make a story of my own organization. The imaginations are pictures of my own organism. For my consciousness to be activated in these images, receptivity of the outer senses and my conscious brain activity must be pushed to the background. In a dimmed state, such as in sleep or focused meditation, we can enter a world of inner self-perception, a world of rich imaginations reflecting, for instance, anabolic metabolism during sleep. These occasionally rise into my consciousness as dreams or pictures with hidden symbolic connotations. In this state we encounter our dreams.

Through the removal of substances from the blood by process of filtration and selective reabsorption, toxic catabolic discards of protein metabolism especially are dissolved in dead water and excreted. The excretion of dead water, which contains the end products of metabolism, helps to regulate the water, electrolyte, and acid-base content of the blood.

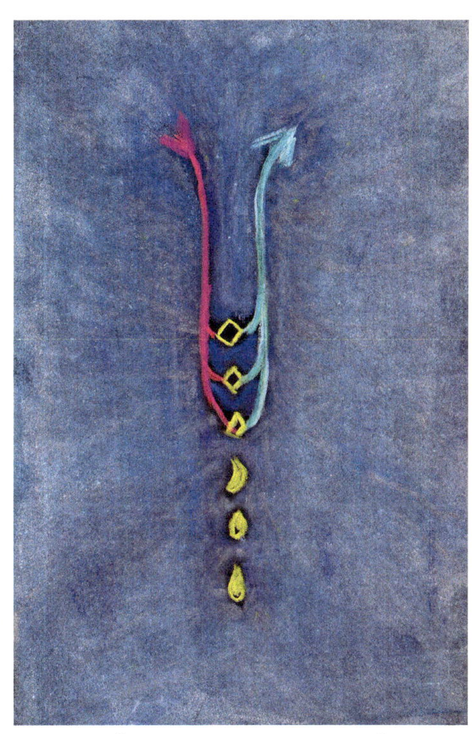

Plate 102: Imagination of living water

As we can gather from the forgoing discussion, the kidney organization in the expression of its formative force, whether warmth ether, light ether, chemical ether, or life ether, supplies one with a rich imagination that can produce a vivid picture for the collective unconscious. Any condition that loosens the adhesive quality between the physical and etheric also conjures subjective phenomena that, on the mental level, are called *schizoid*. Cannabis and LSD are known for their hallucinatory quality when ingested. The weakened physical–etheric bond causes flashbacks, which in turn causes free flowing warmth ether or light ether to circulate and penetrate the consciousness. Here the brain functions as the mirror to the imaginative pictures carried in the etheric organization of the blood.

Kidney radiation can be extremely unpleasant and is in many instances a reason for mental breakdowns and consequently hospitalizations. On the other hand, the kidney personality can lead us into a world of rich images. The books most children have enjoyed and eagerly read emerge from the unconscious weaving of a kidney personality who can analyze and use the rich imagery streaming from the interior to enrich all of us (the *Harry Potter* novels, for example).

Completing the four organs responsible for the construction of all amino-acids in the human being, the scaffolding used by the etheric body is the basic formula constituted of carbon, oxygen, hydrogen and nitrogen (COHN), with multiple permutations thereof. I use an imagination of the substances named atoms and molecules, circulating in the blood from the digestive nutritional stream (*chyle*). The molecular formations are enhanced by each of the four organs through the specific activity of the living water from that organ (being etherized). As a result, an utterly unique protein is enlivened in which the mark of the DNA makes it decisively personal.

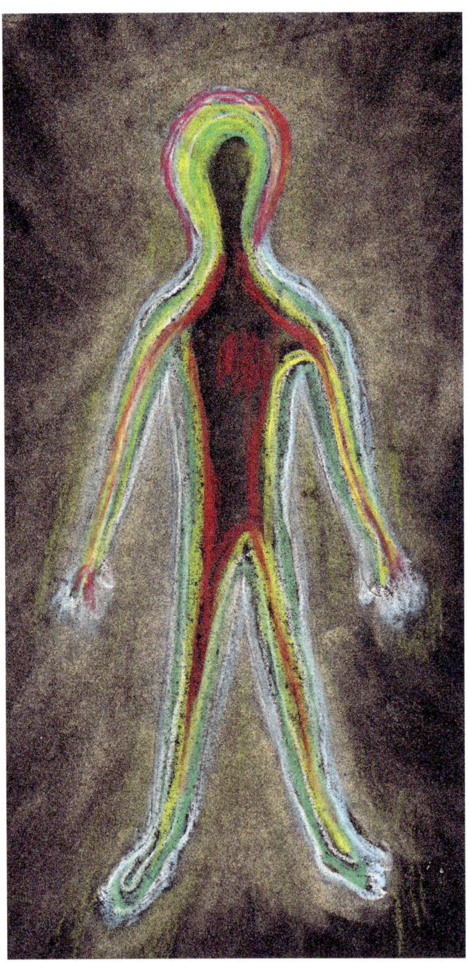

Plate 103: Bonding between physical and etheric

The Heart

Now, let's examine the heart, which adds hydrogen to the formula. We can reflect on the previous organs with this:

earth—lung/carbon
water—liver/oxygen
air—kidney/nitrogen
fire—heart/hydrogen

I feel the order of nature in myself in these fourfold structures and, as an earthling, a certain satisfaction is derived from an exact progression. Can the heart be called an organ? On the physical level, processes of anabolism and catabolism are not identified. The heart is not a pump, though we could call it an organ of propulsion. Branco Furst (*The Heart and Circulation*) shows the essence of the heart function to be more like a hydraulic ram, set into motion by the constant pulsation of the peripheral flow of blood to the center. The heart is made of muscle tissue, and damage to this muscle by vascular impediment or a traumatic contusion results in diminished heart function. Adequate blood flow into muscle tissue is the hallmark for any healthy, active muscle.

The arterial, capillary, and venous parts are integral in the blood-organ circulation. Movement of the blood originates from the periphery and streams via the venous system back to the heart, the center of the circulation. However, I have learned to accept the fact that the heart muscle is not capable of true pump action. One could feel sorry for the heart because of its continuous muscle activity, but if we watch a picture of the electric impulses streaming between contractions it is clear that the heart, of all muscles, chooses its activity judiciously and wisely. Temporally, the contraction (systole) occupies one third of the period (beat), whereas the remaining time is spent in a mode of restoration (diastole). Good for the heart!

And do I have a story? Well, the heart does not have a story. *It is the story!* This story is witnessed in many modern languages as expressed in the synonyms with which we express the purity, courage, warmth, honesty, openness, compassion, tenderness, caring, and sharing of friend and neighbor in our community. The hidden capacity of the heart becomes an experience to the other person, the quality of which is objective. The radiating quality of the heart forces is carried and expressed by the bearer as a light that shines in the dark. It personifies the beauty of humanity, the certainty that evil can be overcome and the hope for a light-filled future. On every level, the story of the heart will become the story of humankind as we are increasingly encouraged to adhere to *The Imitation of Christ* (Thomas à Kempis).

In Latin, the word *cor* is used for the heart, and it is amazing how many modern European words contain this small, three-letter word to express the quality of might and power. Language carries the intimate desires to express those emotions we all want to share.

Have the *cour*age of the Lion when exploring your heart's desire.

The Astral Organization: A Parable

The sequence of events in the life of Christ after the christening by John the Baptist in the River Jordan has been told by many of his disciples, as well as by biographers in the last few centuries. We are not privy to conversations with the friends close to him. What is remarkable is that most of His teachings were conveyed for posterity in the form of parables, from which the reader or listener could extract a message that was meaningful to their own life situation. The prerequisite for such a teaching means that those who receive it are attuned to their own emotional needs, awake to the needs of others, and equipped to discern the vices and virtues with which all humanity would have to deal in earthly life. Institutions of religion have thrived on interpretations of these parables, and for nearly two thousand years desired to think *for* "sinning" human beings.

All personal stories that are made by humans are for humans, and they emerge from the part of the human being we designate the astral body. It is easily remembered that the astral body derives its name from the moving and the fixed stars. Certainly the astrological observations by the priests of the Babylonian civilization (3000 BC) contributed to the wealth of imaginations that have guided humanity's emotional evolution from the primitive aggression of early homo erectus and homo sapiens to the more subtle, civilized, emotionally controlled individuals learning to live in harmony and peace with one another regardless of background.

However, the fact that humanity needs to be reminded repeatedly that we must live according to guidelines, that each vice has a virtue and vice versa, and that each personal effort to control one's emotions becomes the hallmark of maturity, all designates members of humanity as a "work in progress." We are here because we need further exploration. How can emotional maturity be advanced through our own volition and knowledge?

The heavens spoke to Babylonian astrologers thousands of years ago in the "language" of a living, moving world of the animal kingdom. For them it was natural to think of the human being as the center of the universe, **The One,** and that vertical existence is reflected in the planets and the zodiac. Those priests were the namers, and their laws remain valid today.

Here are some of the laws that have been carried into modern star knowledge. Both the moving stars (planets of our solar system) and the fixed stars (members of the zodiacal belt) influence the human being. The body of knowledge associated with this discipline is called *astrology*. The different signs of the zodiac and the planets are dominant at the moment of birth for each person and connote a specific signature.

Plate 104: Enkido embracing the lion

The heavens make a complete circle around the human being in the twenty-four-hour period of one day. The belt of the zodiac is divided into twelve regions, most of them reflecting the signature of an animal. The twelve-month division is earmarked by the calendar months we use in a worldwide order. The fixed stars move slowly around the Earth in a circle of 365 days: one year. The New Year starts at the spring equinox on March 21. This is not a date used as a significant calendar reminder.

At the moment of birth, the configuration of the heavens is imprinted in a child's etheric organization. It is possible that the configuration starts already at the moment of incarnation of **The One** during conception.* For a female child born with a fixed amount of ova, the Sun-Moon angle at birth will determine her ovulatory cycle at the start of reproduction. The Sun-Moon angle will indicate the time of ovulation.

With careful study and observation of animal habits one can frequently notice parallels in the human. The similarity between human profiles and the animal world is a source for humor but can often help us in evaluating peculiarities of our fellow citizens. It is also true that humans living on a farm often take on the characteristics of the animals they care for.

Students of the animal kingdom understand nature's wisdom and how a complete assimilation of the animal in the wild allows it to survive hardships. It is humanization of the animal that makes its survival precarious. The need for closer bonding with the animals has become a curious phenomenon in Western civilization, where members of the animal kingdom, especially our pets, are subjected to human standards.

Cruelty to animals is punishable. An animal in its nature is cruel, but clearly emotional trauma is at a minimum. The capacity for reason in the soul of an animal is absent. When a human being behaves "like an animal," we encounter actions that are despicable, and it is assumed mostly that as a human being "we should know better."

The animal astral body is uncomplicated and rests in its genetic inheritance. In contrast the human astral body, although animal-like in its scaffolding, can be modified, molded through cultivation, and carries responsibility for its reactions in the world.

Human beings are placed on Earth to care for their fellow human beings. But the opposite reaction occurs all too often, leading to war and destruction caused by the overwhelming fact that for

* See, for example, Hilton, *Speaking to the Stars*.

each human being born, the first thought is of the self. The inherent nature of all human beings is centered on the self. It follows that human beings act instinctively from their own insights. Freed from the domination of nature's imprint, the soul activities of thinking, feeling, and will replace the restrictive role of nature and, reaching beyond the animal imprint, create a distinct human activity in which self-thought dominates. Where the animal is incapable of violating natural law and order, human beings regularly overstep natural laws. The following examples will suffice:

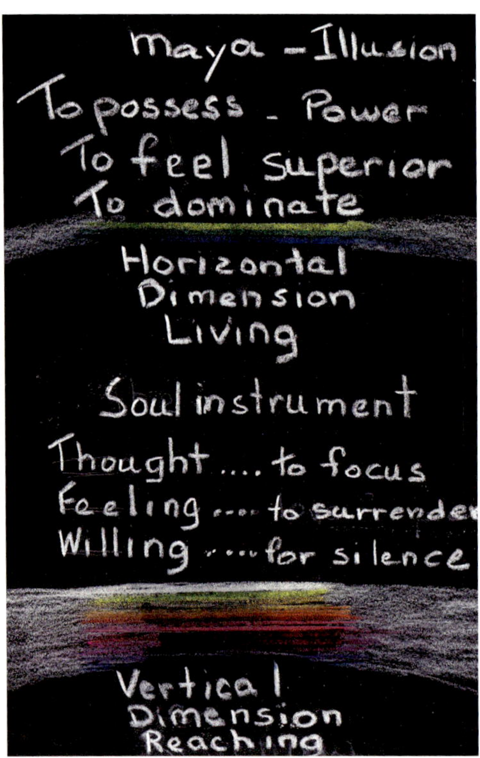

Plate 105: Maya (illusion)

1. Overlooking the world truths, wherein all people are equal. Through seductive and misguided thoughts, appointed leaders of nations are encouraged by their followers to destroy "inferior" factions of humanity. Superiority as a qualitative or quantitative evaluation can be used only in the material, dead world. The living world gives us the challenge to respect the dignity of life.
2. Harboring false and sentimental emotions; the illusion of power and dominance and the willingness to submit to such ideas at the cost of losing our freedom (relinquishing our human freedom to the idea of world power).
3. Belief that the mechanical driven world will triumph. In such a false world, the idea of brother- and sisterhood would be obsolete.

> Slowly the wisdom inherent in nature would be ignored, with resulting destruction of life-sustaining fauna and flora for financial gains and dismissal of the small for the big.

Equality, Freedom, and *Fraternity* were cornerstones of the French Revolution and continued as ideas in the New World when the U.S. Constitution was written.

Conflicts and dysfunction between persons in both private life and in the workplace arise from the array of vices bequeathed to us by the celestial hierarchies. Self-interest dominates; consequently, these vices become challenges, and when consciously emoted, become the configuration of the personal astral body.

We can identify twelve vices, which can be associated with the zodiacal segments present in a 360-degree circumference around us throughout the year. Paul Platt dedicated long years to personal observations regarding the reign of these celestial segments on our astral body and the emotional effects we can observe during waking time (see plate 80, page 117).*

The best defense against negative emotional patterns is the knowledge of one's own human nature or personality. Giving attention to identifying the animal profile within oneself, and learning about the astral patterns and emotions that go unheeded, will bring insight and clarification. Such tools are necessary for the transformation in character, a growth needed in the process of maturing.**

Children learn from fables by identifying with the protagonists. The stories often end with an admonition encouraging the child to become conscious of the plight of the underling, the downtrodden, and the injured or disabled. "The moral of the story is..." Moral standards are introduced, with the recognition that human beings can make choices that are unavailable to animals.

---

* See Platt, "The Quality of Time."

** See Julius, *The Imagery of the Zodiac.*

The astral organization plays a role in the dimension of time (days, months, and years). The rotation of the Earth as planetary body places human beings under continuously changing experiences of cosmic forces throughout the year. To explore these qualities of time with our own inquisitive mind is the hallmark of the human being. It is remarkable that during each minute of waking consciousness an infusion of negative feelings bombards the astral body and, in reality, no one is free of such onslaughts.

What we learn when observing our own comfort or discomfort, the emotions we experience during our confrontations with the world, and the reactions manifested in meeting new circumstances all become the palette of colors we use to paint our biographical tableau. Emotions and reactions become the conscious experience of virtues or vices. We can thank the creative gods for bestowing these hurdles on human beings. My reactions to what comes toward me in this incarnation will determine the path I walk in the future.

As long as the will exists to change, the signs of the zodiac holding the secrets of the vices have been among the best foundations for understanding how to approach personal uncertainties, bolster self-worth, and overcome hurdles in human interactions. Rigidity and separation from " the other" must be resolved to make room for accessibility, affinity, and affability.

The "I" Organization: The Legend

It is at the end of one's life that the world traveler will pose this question: What will I be remembered by? In the eulogy, a review of the memories will inform family, friends, and colleagues of the endearing, brave, and outstanding qualities of a beloved person. There is sadness around the recent separation, but a eulogy is not the legend of the person. Such a story unfolds long after an individuality's sojourn on Earth, allowing the individual time for the review after separating from earthly reality.

Plate 106: Leaving karma behind

The legend has a pure individual expression, and I imagine it will become the garment for the being in the next existence on a different plane, in a new dimension. I do not know the legend that will adorn me in future existence. My legend is an unknown entity, unless it might be connected to the credo I was able to fashion during my contemplations on Earth. It seems to me it becomes important that I was understood as individuality. Have I made myself clear? Was I able to express the confession of my personal convictions in my daily activity? If I had a shimmering of my higher self, could this be conveyed to others? I was able to write down the requirements for writing a credo (the rules of faith I live by) in a previous section. This alone becomes an urgent invitation for **The One** during the daily routine of consistently examining motivations, followed by the question: Are my actions authentic? Am I true to my intentions?

In the act of living, daily gathering is continuous. This action is from periphery to the center. We will all face birth in a new existence. To equip ourselves with a garment of truth, beauty, and goodness becomes a goal for our present earthly life. These are the contributions with which we will enter a new existence. What will be the garment?

I bring here a final story of transition, witnessed in one of my patients. While on his deathbed there came a defining moment when he threw off his covers, slipped out of his bed, stood erect holding on to the table for stability, and with one last breath expressed in a loud voice, "I want to be free!" At that moment his transition became a reality; he excarnated. While leaving the realm of Earth, the horizontal plane, he was fully conscious and able to step eagerly into another existence without fear or uncertainty. Was this his legend?

Once we can leave the restrictive earthly body, a journey through our universe can be undertaken and expressed in terms of an expansion. The progression is orderly, following a path similar to our path of travel during sleep. Every seven years, further and higher. The spheres of Moon, Mercury, Venus, Sun, Mars, Jupiter, and Saturn are all visited and are represented in ever-increasing intensity of light and illumination. I imagine that the hierarchies in these celestial spheres are occupied with nothing but expanding the understanding of the individual—understanding the functions and form connected with the physical body. This becomes the knowing with which **The One** will return to repeat the cycle and reconnect with the beloved *Sophia–Gaya*.

My daily life is occupied with the thoughts of the past, present, and future. Thoughts of people I was destined to meet and the changes I have witnessed, specifically the deleterious effects on the youth, have spurred me on to impart my concerns and apprehensions of what might be of help for the future. In this way I hope to contribute to a process of curiosity and awakening **The One** in the reader.

Epilogue

Knowledge of my existence as infinite is a reality given to me through grace at such a young age that it was not shared or questioned. As my life unfolded, many encounters, memories, and stories with other human beings have accumulated, giving birth to this testimony of **The One** weaving the intricate pattern of destiny on our planet Earth.

The introduction of a belief system was unacceptable, and I had no need for adherence to doctrines, most of which thrive on sentiments of superiority. The concept of "belief" creates uncertainties in all decisions one has to make. On the other hand a "knowing" deep within my heart has provided me with an empowerment for daily activities throughout my life.

All that I learned from my studies was not only memorized but also integrated into a scaffolding of realities and became acceptable truths. I followed a voice within, nudging me to differentiate between "the tree and the woods." The question of who spoke with an unassailable guiding voice within me became the leading motive for an investigation into suprasensory realities, the acquisition of which I assigned to a vertical plane. The curiosity for such knowledge has continued to accompany me throughout my studies and in the life journey I have been privileged to undertake. It is curious that in the seven-year stages of my life new certainties emerged from the "sea of unknowing" to enrich the horizontal life I was living beyond the mundane.

It was only after the age of forty-two that my continuous inquiry surrounding a dominating figure mentioned in stories of evolution throughout the world, was answered and solidified in my own mind. Testimony of a visitation to our planet by an avatar needed to be explored.

The writings of Édouard Schuré (*The Initiates*) and Rudolf Steiner (*The Gospel of John*) illumined my path toward the certainty that Christ, as a fiery alien light-being who claimed a human body, walked the Earth for three years, left a body of teachings transmitted through the Bible, and remains deeply connected with humankind. This became a new overarching reality in my life. Sentiments of infinite allegiance and the riddle of how to validate such a discovery in day-consciousness stirred my daily activity.

This life-shaking conversion ripened over a seven-year period, finalizing in the realization that opposing forces, destructive, seductive, and evil, do exist and continually lure **The One** away from possibilities of spontaneous allegiance to the God-spark in all of us. I heeded the voice reminding me that the lonely path of individual action needs to be recognized.

Yes, I now experienced being alone but never lonely. The voice has accompanied me throughout time and space. I trusted it, obeyed suggestions that were sometimes scary, and found succor in knowing the unswerving fidelity and love for me.

My practice shifted from the conventional methods of internal medicine, in which quantitative evaluations are encouraged. Pursuing a quality in the consulting hour demanded that all members of a family were introduced. I was repeatedly challenged to practice a medical art that is extended by wisdom of the human being in its truthful representation of an evolving body, soul, and spirit. The new patient entering this sphere of healing often made a conscious choice to work toward a self-recovery and demanded control of the healing process.

Such an interaction opened new worlds to me, introduced ideas of support in the impulse of self-healing, and acquainted me with age-old philosophies and knowledge to which the modern medical student is not privy.

The tenacious execution of methods in healing with which I had been unfamiliar until that time required trust, self-reliance, and enormous courage. Developing my own spiritual discipline and creating a pathway for "help from above" was a mandate in this process of growth.

What I came to realize is that Christianized medicine begins with each of my patients, the moment it was recognized that the empowerment for healing is inherent within the patient.

The individual is a work in progress. Mechanical medical intervention interferes with self-healing. Being sick calls for introspection by the patient eventually guided by the "healer." In this process, support from finely diluted (homeopathic) substances derived from nature facilitates restoration of the balance needed.

The One is not alone. The four kingdoms it experiences on the horizontal plane surround it. From the celestial spheres, it receives continuous support in thought forms of constructive guidance and affection. This world speaks in me; I will be introduced to it only when I allow room to hear the voice. Our mandate is to listen. A path of understanding leads to freedom.

The introduction of the Child Artist in my life and the work that was prepared by him for all of humanity was a voice of the modern, searching human. On an unconscious level, he was persistent in not allowing his message to slip into nothingness. To do so meant a sacrificial act, experiencing hell through the path of substance abuse and poison.

The human interaction between the "healer" and the "patient" is continuously interchanging. We end with the question: Who heals? This is answered with the certainty that each human being becomes the medicine and remedy for the "other."

Could this fact prepare us for a future where compassion as a spontaneous function of the heart will develop?

See me

Feel me

Touch me

Heal me...

—The Who, *Tommy*

Cited & Recommended Reading

Alexander, Eben. *Proof of Heaven: A Neurosurgeon's Journey into the Afterlife.* New York: Simon and Schuster, 2012.

Anonymous. *Meditations on the Tarot: A Journey into Christian Hermeticism.* Trans. Robert Powell. New York: TarcherPerigee, 2002.

Appenzeller, Kaspar. *Genesis in the Light of Human Embryonic Development.* Spencertown, NY: SteinerBooks, 2022.

Blechschmidt, Erich. *The Beginnings of Human Life.* New York: Springer, 1977.

Boogert, Arie. *What Happens after We Die: Making the Connection between the Living and the Dead.* Spencertown, NY: Lindisfarne Books 2021

Cockren, A. *History of Alchemy from Ancient Egypt to Modern Times.* http://alchemylab.com/history_of_alchemy.htm.

Dunselman, Ron. *In Place of the Self: How Drugs Work.* Stroud, UK: Hawthorn, 1993.

Emerson, Ralph Waldo. *Essays: First and Second Series.* New York: Harper Perennial, 1951.

Furst, Branko, MD. *The Heart and Circulation: An Integrative Model.* New York: Springer, 2014.

Hilton, Jonathan. *Speaking to the Stars: An Introduction to Astrosophy.* Spencertown, NY: Lindisfarne Books, 2023.

Husemann, Armin J. *Form, Life, and Consciousness: An Introduction to Anthroposophic Medicine and Study of the Human Being.* Spencertown, NY: SteinerBooks, 2019.

———. *The Harmony of the Human Body: Musical Principles in Human Physiology.* Edinburgh: Floris Books, 2003.

———. *What Makes Blood Move? A Mind-Body Physiology of the Heart.* Spencertown, NY: SteinerBooks, 2022.

Jenny, Hans. *Cymatics; A Study of Wave Phenomena and Vibration,* 3rd ed. Eliot, ME: MACROmedia, 2001.

Jocelyn, Beredene. *Citizens of the Cosmos: Life's Unfolding from Conception through Death to Rebirth.* Great Barrington, MA: SteinerBooks, 2009.

Julius, Frits H. *The Imagery of the Zodiac.* Edinburgh: Floris Books, 1993.

Kempis, Thomas à. *The Imitation of Christ.* Brooklyn: Confraternity of the Precious Blood, 2014.

Klocek, Dennis. *The Alchemical Wedding: Christian Rosenkreutz, the Initiate of Misunderstanding.* Spencertown, NY: Lindisfarne Books, 2021.

———. *Colors of the Soul: Physiological and Spiritual Qualities of Light and Dark*. Great Barrington, MA: Lindisfarne Books, 2017.

König, Karl, MD. *Embryology and World Evolution*. Freiburg: Verlag die Kommenden, 2000.

Lauterwasser, Alexander. *Water Sound Images: The Creative Music of the Universe*. Encinitas, CA: MACROmedia, 2007.

Maintier, Serge. *Speech—Invisible Creation in the Air: Vortices and the Enigma of Speech Sounds*. Ed. R. Patzlaff. Great Barrington, MA: SteinerBooks, 2016 (see also Johanna Zinke).

McAllen, Audrey. *The Extra Lesson: Movement, Drawing, and Painting Exercises to Help Children with Difficulties in Writing, Reading, and Arithmetic*. Fair Oaks, CA: Rudolf Steiner College, 2018.

McGraw, Jamie. "The Life and Legacy of Hermes Trismegistus." *Alchemy Journal*, vol. 3, no. 4, 2002.

Nahm, Michael. *Wenn die Dunkelheit ein Ende findet: Terminale Geistesklarheit und andere ungewöhnliche Phänomene in Todesnähe* (When the darkness comes to an end: Terminal mental clarity and other unusual phenomena near death). Amerang, Germany: Crotona, 2012.

O'Neil, George, and Gisela O'Neil. *The Human Life*. Chestnut Ridge, NY: Mercury Press, 1990.

Platt, Paul. "The Quality of Time." Self-published essay, 1982.

Reich, Wilhelm. *The Function of the Orgasm: Sex-economic Problems of Biological Energy*. New York: Farrar, Straus and Giroux, 1973.

Rittelmeyer, Friedrich. *Reincarnation: A Christian Perspective* (3rd ed.). Edinburgh: Floris, 2018.

Roob, Alexander. *Alchemy and Mysticism*. Berlin: Taschen, 2014.

Schuré, Édouard. *The Great initiates: A Study of the Secret History of Religions*. Great Barrington, MA: SteinerBooks, 1989.

Schwaller de Lubicz, RA. *The Temple in Man: Sacred Architecture and the Perfect Man*. Rochester, VT: Inner Traditions, 1977.

Södergran, Edith. *Love and Solitude: Selected Poems, 1916–1923*. Translated by Stina Katchadourian. Fjord Press 1981.

Steiner, Rudolf. *Anthroposophical Leading Thoughts: Anthroposophy as a Path of Knowledge: The Michael Mystery* (CW [Collected Works] 26). Forest Row, UK: Rudolf Steiner Press, 1973.

———. *Awakening to Community* (CW 257). Spring Valley, NY: Anthroposophic Press, 1975.

———. *The Challenge of the Times* (CW 186). Spring Valley, NY: Anthroposophic Press, 1979.

———. *Christianity as Mystical Fact: And the Mysteries of Antiquity* (CW 8). Great Barrington, MA: SteinerBooks, 1997.

———. *Eurythmy as Speech Made Visible: Speech Eurythmy Course* (CW 279). Forest Row, UK: Rudolf Steiner Press, 2024.

———. *Freemasonry and Ritual Work: The Misraim Service* (CW 265). Great Barrington, MA: SteinerBooks, 2007.

———. *The Gospel of John* (CW 103). Spencertown, NY: SteinerBooks, 2022.

———. *How to Know Higher Worlds: A Modern Path of Initiation* (CW 10). Hudson, NY: Anthroposophic Press, 1994.

———. *Intuitive Thinking as a Spiritual Path: A Philosophy of Freedom* (CW 4). Hudson, NY: Anthroposophic Press, 1995.

———. *Man and the World of Stars: The Spiritual Communion of Mankind* (CW 219). New York: Anthroposophic Press, 1982.

———. *Occult History: Historical Personalities and Events in the Light of Spiritual Science* (CW 126). London: Rudolf Steiner Press, 1982.

———. *An Occult Physiology* (CW 128). Forest Row, UK: Rudolf Steiner Press, 1997.

———. *An Outline of Esoteric Science* (CW 13). Hudson, NY: Anthroposophic Press, 1997.

———. *A Psychology of Body, Soul, and Spirit: Anthroposophy, Psychosophy, Pneumatosophy* (CW 115). Hudson, NY: Anthroposophic Press, 1999.

———.*Theosophy: An Introduction to the Spiritual Processes in Human Life and in the Cosmos* (CW 9). Hudson, NY: Anthroposophic Press, 1994.

Unger, Carl. *The Language of the Consciousness Soul: A Guide to Rudolf Steiner's "Leading Thoughts."* Great Barrington, MA: SteinerBooks, 2012.

———. *Steiner's Theosophy and Principles of Spiritual Science.* Great Barrington, MA: SteinerBooks, 2014.

Van der Bie, Guus, MD. *Embryology: Early Development from a Phenomenological Point of View.* Driebergen, The Netherlands: Louis Bolk, 2001.

Weldon, Laura Grace. "Mother and Child Are Linked at the Cellular Level." https://lauragraceweldon.com/2012/06/12/mother-child-are-linked-at-the-cellular-level (2012).

Wolff, Otto, MD. *Grundlagen einer geisteswissenschaftlich erweiterten Biochemie* (Basics of biochemistry expanded from the humanities). Stuttgart: Verlag Freies Geistesleben, 2013.

Zinke, Johanna. *Luftlautformen* (The air vowel form). Gerabronn, Germany: Hohenloher Druck, 1978 (see Serge Maintier).

Zuccoli, Elena. *Tone and Speech Eurythmy.* Edinburgh: Floris Books 2023.

Index of Plates

Acknowledgments

The autobiography of a professional woman in a new country is studded with meetings positive as well as negative. All encounters have contributed to the embroidery of my own life journey and molding.

My first friend, Diana, initially a buddy on the ski slope, soon came to share her family, home, and table in spontaneous gestures of hospitality so typical of the old Italian roots present in our community. The warm embrace of welcome seemed to be most prominent with those folks who counted immigrants from the Mediterranean regions as their forebears. Eddy and Cathy Stiffler became friends, neighbors, and confidants throughout the time of acquiring the farm and beyond. Without Craig Schools' filiality toward the animals on our farm, my expression as a farmer would not have been possible. The folks who always stood by my side include Leah, Joanna, Judy, Joyce, and Melissa. I cannot imagine being without their enduring patience and loyalty.

My writings and impressions on life have been formed by the review of my peers and friends whose input I appreciate. Outstanding meetings I value and appreciate with the younger generations that have come before me. Starting in the 1960s, the incarnating souls reflected an astounding evolution. They showed interest, curiosity, and an iron will to complete the task they set out to do. My son Peter Pupator is one of them, and I feel profound gratitude for his dedication also to the material that was really a part of my story. Alex Schneider, always willing to give jovial contributions, brought me through the times of despondency with my inadequate control of the computer screen. All these, my younger friends Michael, Stacey, Heidi, Andrew, and Arthur, I have understood, and they in return have lightened my way.

Encouragement to make my own blackboard drawings, where possible, came from a wonderful artist herself, Sylvia Hough. She especially captured the moods of the texts, and her contributions beautify this testimony. I thank her for plates 27, 29, 30, 37, 39, 40, 48, 72, 74, 83, and 94.

The generation born in the nineties contributed in a new way. These young and often prominent incarnated souls did not ask for personal attention. Being able to carry them in my consciousness awakened in me the eagerness to share the results of the maze in which my life unfolded. Certainly the Child Artist gave me a reward by sharing his artistic story in spite of his own struggle to find meaning in his life. This generation has something to say, and they remind us to listen.